KICK AND RUN

D0615749

KICK AND RUN

Memoir with Soccer Ball

JONATHAN WILSON

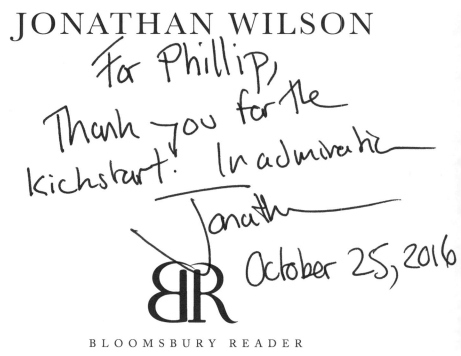

For Phillip,
Thank you for the
kickstart! In admiration

Jonath

October 25, 2016

BLOOMSBURY READER

LONDON · NEW DELHI · NEW YORK · SYDNEY

This edition published in 2013 by Bloomsbury Reader

Bloomsbury Reader is a division of Bloomsbury Publishing Plc,

50 Bedford Square, London WC1B 3DP

First published in Great Britain 2013 by Bloomsbury Reader

Copyright © 2013 Jonathan Wilson

All rights reserved

You may not copy, distribute, transmit, reproduce or otherwise
make available this publication (or any part of it) in any form, or by any means
(including without limitation electronic, digital, optical, mechanical, photocopying,
printing, recording or otherwise), without the prior written permission of the
publisher. Any person who does any unauthorised act in relation to this publication
may be liable to criminal prosecution and civil claims for damages

The moral right of the author is asserted

ISBN: 978 1 4482 1378 8
eISBN: 978 1 4482 1253 8

Visit www.bloomsburyreader.com to find out more about our authors and their books
You will find extracts, author interviews, author events and you can sign up for
newsletters to be the first to hear about our latest releases and special offers
Printed and bound in the U.S.A by Thomson-Shore Inc., Dexter, Michigan

For John Bailey

My over-excitement was beyond all description

Jules Verne

Kick and Run is a work of memoir. It reflects the author's present recollection of his experiences over a period of many years. Certain names, locations and identifying characteristics have been changed. Dialogue and events have been recreated from memory and, in some cases, have been compressed to convey the substance of what was said or what occurred.

Contents

Pre-Game

In May and June of 2006 I spent a few weeks in the almost unbearably charming French village of Talloires, where Churchill liked to summer, and from whose terraced hillside Cézanne once painted a castle that sits on the opposite side of Lake Annecy. It is true that I was drinking a lot of wine on those chilly Haute-Savoie nights, but alcohol, it turned out, was not what was precipitating my weekly falls from bed.

Here's the thing: each time I catapulted to the floor I was mid-dream, executing a spectacular soccer move, an overhead or scissor kick, a delirious pivot and shoot, a spectacular leap over two defenders. My muscles, which were supposed to be asleep, twitched into action, and fabulous spasms sent me flying, arms and legs akimbo, into the unforgiving furniture of my bedroom. Once I cracked my head so violently on the bedside table that I was rendered briefly unconscious, as if Manny Pacquiao had struck me with a fierce left hook.

I had suspected for some time that soccer was deeply embedded in my unconscious, but I had not realized how frequently it populated my dreams until its fitful eruptions abbreviated my sleep.

Back home in the States, the episodes increased in frequency, such that after a few months I was sleeping like a big baby, with "bumpers" in the shape of numerous pillows placed around the bed in case I threw myself into action during some vital World Cup game. This continued for two years until one night I moved right instead of left and inadvertently whacked my wife in the head with a flying elbow. I made an appointment with my doctor.

A few weeks before I crashed out for the first time in Talloires, I had begun to take small daily doses of the anti-depressant Zoloft; this medication had been prescribed to me by a shrink who, I'd felt from the beginning of our acquaintance, did not like me very much. She seemed to disapprove of everything I said and did, and, like my older brothers before her, generally sided with whomever it was that I was whining about.

I was only with this shrink, let's call her Dr. Scold, because after seven years of analysis I had finally told my previous shrink, Dr. Kind, how much I hated her knee-high stockings, published a story in *Esquire* that reiterated the session, and then felt so guilty that I'd decided to quit. Dr. Kind was of the opinion that pretty much everything I directed at her was intended for my mother. This may well have been so, although the possibility also exists that Freud, as the novelist Saul Bellow once remarked, was a nudnik who subjugated us with powerful metaphors.

Before I went to see my doctor, the respected author of a self-published guide to good living called "Don't Worry, Be Healthy," I searched WebMD for an explanation of my symptoms, and what I came up with was illuminating. Certain SSRI drugs, of which Zoloft is one, have been known to bring on neo-epileptic symptoms during REM sleep, like those I had experienced while playing dream-soccer. I described what I had discovered to my doctor, and he said, "Stop taking the Zoloft." Dr. Scold weaned me slowly and carefully off the little blue pills, and my symptoms gradually disappeared. When I had stopped falling out of bed altogether, I e-mailed Dr. Scold and told her that I thought I might now proceed without her services. True to form, she never replied.

Sometimes I miss my extravagant propulsions. I don't play soccer anymore, and if I dream of it I rarely remember having done so. But I would guess that, unless things have changed dramatically, many of my sleeping hours, like a great deal of my waking hours, are spent observing the same field of dreams, 100 yards by 50 yards, twenty-two players, white lines, a center circle, goalposts, a net, and, waiting to be ecstatically smacked past a flying goalkeeper's outstretched arms, that universal orb, the soccer ball.

First Half

Chapter 1

I am six years old and walking with my father to the flower gardens at the summit of Gladstone Park. I like the dwarf hedges there, which make me feel tall, and the stone sundial. It takes us a long time to reach the gardens because my father stops frequently to rest his weary heart. It is Saturday afternoon. When we arrive and enter through the trellised gate heavy with ivy, we see Rabbi Rabinowitz and his son David sitting on a bench next to a freshly trimmed yew tree. The rabbi and my father are still in the same dark suits they have worn to synagogue that morning. I have a tennis ball in my pocket. I have kicked it through the park, running ahead of my father to retrieve and kick it again. David gets up and stands about ten feet away from me, facing me without speaking. I put the ball on the ground and side-foot it toward him. Frozen rigid, he makes no move. He isn't allowed to play with a ball on the Sabbath. The ball rolls into an undergrowth beneath the yew tree. I search but I can't find it. I'm not sure if my father is embarrassed that he has allowed me to come into the park with a ball, or if it is all right.

The four of us walk back downhill, past the drinking fountain, past the swings, past the soccer changing rooms, over the railway bridge near the allotments, past the refreshment booth and out of the park. The rabbi and my father in front, then me bouncing and kicking an imaginary ball, then David, trailing along the path.

* * *

I harbored few illusions, even as a child, that I could become a professional soccer player, but this certainly didn't prevent me either from indulging in extravagant soccer fantasies, "It's Wilson … for England … he scores!!!!" or from playing every chance I got. My career began in Gladstone Park, a picturesque green space bisected by a railway line that occupied several acres behind my house in Dollis Hill, a suburb in North West London. Frequently, as I walked from Helena Road to Park Avenue and approached the two giant oaks that God had set precisely eight yards apart for use as a goal, I watched from a distance as happy, frolicking ten- to fifteen-year-olds kicked the ball, so lively and high-stepping that they might have been dancing round a maypole. Proximity, however, told a different story. The running boys were my friends, but all too often a pride of local thugs was in pursuit, members of the vicious Chapter Road gang, who had 1) stolen our ball, and 2) were about to throw someone to the ground and assault him with kicks and bicycle chains. Somewhere between the essence and the descent fell the shadow.

I lived on a street where all but two families were middle-class Jews, like us, the Wilsons, formerly the Wilsicks until, after almost a decade of pressure from my mother, my father changed his name in 1940. His father, Wolf, an alive but absent presence in my life whom I only met once, had arrived in England as Wilczyk in 1904.

8

From the age of five I attended Gladstone Park Primary School, a five minute walk from our home. At first my brother Stephen, six years my senior, (my oldest brother Geoffrey, 21 when I was five, had been conscripted into the army for two years) took me to school in the morning, a journey intermittently as fraught as the soccer games in the park. In a brilliant stroke of town planning the local authorities had situated the reform school for local delinquents in the heart of our middle class neighborhood, while the "nice" school for local kids of all stripes was located on the edge of a tough neighborhood. Thus, the schools' respective students had to cross paths every morning and afternoon. The hard kids were not fond of the middle class kids, and held a special animus towards Jews. Once, on the way to school, a group of them stopped my brother and me. They ignored me but held Stephen up against a wall and singed his eyebrows with a cigarette lighter. I said, plaintively, "Leave my brother alone," but of course they just laughed. Afterwards Stephen grew angry with me, but how could he not? There was no one else around to soak up the humiliation and the pain.

The year I turned ten, I was appointed captain of the school soccer team by our form master and coach, Mr. Fielding. Mr. Fielding knew very little about soccer; he was far better at compelling our interest in adventure stories by reading aloud in class from John Buchan's *Prester John* and H. Rider Haggard's *King Solomon's Mines*, novels that later in life it was disappointing to discover were salient examples of the worst of British imperial arrogance and racism. There were forty children in our class; those who came, quite literally, from the wrong side of the tracks (the Bakerloo tube line ran aboveground outside our classroom windows) frequently had holes in their sweaters and shoes, and looked like the Dickensian poor. When a Jamaican boy, Jarvis

Campbell, was introduced to the room, it was the first time any of us had ever seen a black child our own age in person before. Jarvis's family was part of a small first wave of immigrants moving to London from the West Indies. Several of us happily wore Sambo-like golliwog pins—enamel collectibles redeemable from Robertson's jams and marmalades—on our sweaters and lapels. During break the girls took turns stroking Jarvis's hair.

Gladstone Park Primary School played in yellow and green quartered shirts. Our home field was in the park, where the "changing rooms" were tiny huts whose amenities consisted of two benches illuminated by a single light-bulb and a communal cold-water sink. In the season that I was captain, we lost every game except the final one against our local rivals, Mora Road. Our school had some tough kids, but Mora Road was completely committed to the hard life. After we had taken a 2–0 lead, a group of Mora Road's harshest ruffians simply lined up on their bicycles about an inch behind their goal line (there were posts and a crossbar, but no nets). It was a brilliant move: we could no longer aim at the goal, for if the ball hit one of their bikes it would provide the required excuse to beat the shit out of us after the match was over. Of course they didn't really need an excuse, but it was thoughtful of them to pretend that they did. Mr. Fielding, as always, had gone home at halftime. He had a long commute.

Despite Gladstone Park's poor performances, I was selected, by whom I never knew, for team trials to play for my local London district, Willesden. In those years, Willesden (of which Dollis Hill constituted a part) was a middle-middle, lower-middle, and working-class neighborhood of Jewish bakers, Greek-Cypriot barbers, and Irish laborers. Forty years later, when Zadie Smith, also a Willesdener, put it on the map with her pyrotechnic novel *White Teeth*, the Jews and the Greeks were long gone, replaced on the roster of immigrants by Asians and West Indians.

Unfortunately, the October match to determine selection for Willesden U12 was scheduled for Yom Kippur. In places with large Jewish populations, like New York City or Newton, Massachusetts, where I have lived for the last twenty-seven years, and where local public schools are closed on the Jewish Day of Atonement, such a conflict could never occur, but in England, Jewish sensibilities are not so delicately attended to, and my participation in the trial was not even up for debate.

I was profoundly disappointed not to try out for Willesden. But the footballing heart of a ten-year-old is resilient, and when the autumn Jewish festivals ended, I made a bold move. Each week I read two comics, *The Lion* and *The Tiger*. *The Tiger* featured the soccer superstar Roy of the Rovers, who played for Melchester, a team clearly based on Manchester United. *The Lion*, however, included a column in which readers could advertise their own nascent soccer leagues and search for other teams to play. I created Gladstone Park Rangers, and I even wrote to the Football Association, England's governing soccer authority, and someone in their organization wrote back an encouraging letter. We had sticks for goals, no crossbar, and no net. We played on an unmarked field in an area of Gladstone Park not officially designated for soccer, there was no referee, and yet other teams, informal collectives of neighborhood kids from different parts of the city, traveled to play us. No parents or coaches were involved at all. It was surpassingly great.

My school friend, David Feldman, a goalkeeper whose father was a socialist and not an observant Jew like mine, did get permission to try out for Willesden. Though he didn't make the

11

team, Feldman was as soccer-obsessed as I was. That winter we played Subbuteo, the hands-on precursor to Nintendo's *FIFA Soccer 10*, in his family's dining room. We unrolled the green baize field on the table, set up goals, corner flags, and spectators, chose our teams, and passed hours deftly flicking the tiny weighted figures onto and around the plastic ball, passing, shooting, scoring.

The following spring, for reasons that elude me to this day, my friend decided to torment me: he persuaded all the boys in my class to stop talking to me, and insult to injury, he stole my cap! My father was sick, his heart condition had recently worsened, and perhaps my response to this new phase of his illness presented some heightened vulnerability in me that my peers, like predatory animals, sensed and could not resist exploiting.

I spent the last months of elementary school in something close to monastic silence, my only friend another rejected boy, Julian Fazler, a kind-hearted nerd before there were nerds. At one point, Feldman offered me a way out. If I would agree to fight (i.e., get beaten up by) Brian Lundin, the toughest kid in the school, I could return to the group, credentials intact. I declined the offer.

My mother wanted to know what had happened to my cap. Eventually, I told her, and she went to the Feldman house and retrieved it. She wasn't surprised by the theft. She considered the Feldmans at least one rung below us on the social ladder—Mr. Feldman was a tailor—and it galled her to no end when, eight years on, David got into Oxford and I didn't.

* * *

In his poignant essay *The Crack-Up*, Scott Fitzgerald counted his failure to make the (American) football team at Princeton the first of two juvenile regrets of his life. (The other was not getting overseas during WWI.) Yet, in the end, from these twin frustrations evolved the deep understanding of illusion and disillusion that inform his greatest work.

If Fitzgerald had made the football team at Princeton, I doubt there would have been a Jay Gatsby. I'm not saying that if I'd made the Willesden soccer team in 1960 I wouldn't have tried to become a writer, but certainly lessons in disappointment must play some part in forging a creative sensibility.

The philosopher Jacques Derrida is another case in point. In response to a question about whether he ever did anything "normal" in his life, like "go to the movies or play sports," Derrida replied: "You've touched a private part of me ... I wanted to be a professional soccer player, but I had to give it up because I was not good enough." As with Fitzgerald, we have Derrida's relative ineptitude on the muddy fields of glory and his subsequent surrender to the lessons of the real to thank for the entire magnificent invisible city of his (de)constructions.

According to the supremely inventive Russian formalist critic and novelist Viktor Shklovsky, this kind of sublimation, whether it takes the form of unrealized ambition or unrequited love, is probably responsible for most of humankind's cultural achievements. Shklovsky himself fashioned a formidable experimental novel, *Zoo or Letters not About Love*, out of his failure to persuade his beloved, Elsa Triolet, to return his feelings in kind. Fitzgerald, too, said he wrote *The Beautiful and the Damned* "to get the girl."

Presumably this all goes back to hunting. Adolescent boys I knew in London used to refer to their Friday night peregrinations in search of suitable female partners as "going on the 'unt," while soccer has frequently been designated by anthropologists as a late-coming incarnation of the prehistoric hunting party, where teamwork and slinging stones were essential for a good kill. But what if, like some ten-thousand-year-old Fitzgerald or Derrida on the African savannah, you were lousy at hunting? Well, most likely you went back to the fire to entertain the women, got them to gather round and warm their hands while you sat upon the ground and told sad tales of the death of kings.

Of course, failure doesn't always work out so advantageously. My cousin Cheryl, who lived in Neville's Court at the top of Gladstone Park, from whose vantage she had a magnificent view of the great, green, windswept expanses of at least three soccer fields, wanted to be a ballerina, and raged against her short and dumpy but otherwise accommodating and sweet parents for years on account of the gene pool they had assigned her by mating and which, in Cheryl's case, had created a figure light on its feet, but, sadly, eminently resistible to corps de ballet worldwide. First she *taught* ballet, always a downer, and then she went into IT, only to despair of that broad but denatured avenue and return to her first love, to run the box office at Sadler's Wells while long-legged girls, the daughters of tall, slender Nordic parents, slipped their dainty shoulders in and out of the stage doors.

In the England of my childhood, no Jewish person, as far as I was aware, played in the top tier of professional soccer (in France, Derrida clearly thought he might be the first), and it was not until 1979 that the situation changed, when an Israeli, Avi Cohen, joined Liverpool FC. Even if Avi had arrived earlier, everyone knows that in the matter of sports, Israelis cannot count as role models for young Diaspora Jews—which is not to say that I did not venerate a Jewish soccer god in my childhood. I did, and his name was Miles Spector.

In the democratic 1950s and early 1960s, amateur soccer had

a large following in post-war, entertainment-starved England, and the Amateur Cup Final held at the country's premiere soccer stadium, Wembley, with its magnificent twin towers, drew crowds of up to 60,000. My brother Geoffrey, who couldn't have been less interested in soccer, was nevertheless kind enough to take me, with his friend Noel Gellman, to one of these finals: Hendon (a neighborhood only two or three miles from our house) v. Kingstonian. Miles Spector played for Hendon, in the unglamorous Isthmian League (there were amateur leagues all over London named for the glories of ancient Greece: Athenian, Corinthian, and, following suit, the Ionian League, invented by my friend Richard Tucker for Gladstone Park Rangers and its adversaries. He drew impressive columns and caryatids for the championship certificates). Miles Spector was Hendon's burly center forward, a prolific goal scorer with both foot and head, and, as everyone had mentioned to me at least four hundred times since I had announced that I was going to the Hendon v. Kingstonian game, yes, Miles Spector was Jewish!

But even becoming Miles Spector was clearly out of reach. You had to be a Christian god to play professional soccer; a Jewish deity could apparently rise through the ranks in the amateur leagues (years later I learned that Miles Spector had, in fact, played six times for Chelsea, a superhuman achievement), but a mere Jewish boy from Willesden? Fuggedabahtit.

Jacques Derrida or Zinedine Zidane? Whose cultural impact has been greater? In deference to Derrida, we must eschew the either/or. Enough to know he wanted to be Zidane.

Chapter 2

My father, Lewis, was one of those decent, conative individuals who strove through hard and disciplined work to
keep his family intact and make ends meet. After a brief stab at
rabbinical school, he had taken a junior administrative position
in the offices of the United Synagogue of Great Britain, the
same institution for which he had begun his working life as an
elevator boy while in his mid-teens. He quickly rose through the
ranks to become the company secretary, a higher post than it
sounds. He got to the office early and he left late. He was always
conservatively and carefully dressed and coiffed, and he exhib-
ited a combination of quiet dignity and secure knowledge that
made him the go-to man in our neighborhood on any number
of matters, and especially those relating to the proper conduct of
an observant London Jewish life. The only splash of color he
permitted himself in his clothing generally resided in the bowties
he liked to wear.

Once, when I was in a Boston hospital after receiving a soccer-
related injury that had turned my right leg black from ankle to
knee, my primary care physician, a Harvard man, came to visit
me. He too specialized in striking bowtie neckwear. My

roommate, a roofer who had accidentally severed three fingers on his right hand with a chainsaw and was presently high as a kite on some kind of morphine-Oxycontin cocktail, took one look at my PCP and said, "What's with the fucking bowtie?" I wouldn't have thought to ask my father this question, although I have come to believe that it is almost always a good one.

My father thought England the best country in the world: tolerant, refined, and surpassingly civilized. As a self- and night-school-taught intellectual, he enjoyed reading quality literature, and our bookshelves were stocked not only with great English writers from Shakespeare to D. H. Lawrence, but also, as my father knew German, with Schiller, Goethe, and Heine in the original. As a young man, his recreational pursuits included tennis, hiking, and possibly motorcycling in the countryside—I say possibly because I own an improbable photograph of my father, oversized goggles lifted to his forehead, on an impressive AJS motorcycle in front of two Monet-like haystacks circa 1926, and the shot has the absolute feel of a one-off. Art, theater, literature,

philosophy, politics, Jewish thought, history, prayer and observance, music, film—all these were in his repertoire.

My father suffered from a heart condition bequeathed him by a childhood bout with rheumatic fever, and by early middle age, he was an invalid: a man who could not surmount the softest undulation without pausing for breath. He loved to garden, and he continued to do so long after his heart disease had dictated that he should stop. My mother would lean out of the kitchen window and yell "Lew, enough! Stop!" but my father, spade or heavy fork in hand, kept digging and turning the earth in preparation for planting.

When I was very young, I had watched him construct a new fence between our backyard and our neighbor's. He sawed planks, dug a trench, established the plumb line, and, my favorite part, applied creosote to the wood. Once the fence was in place, he tended to the plants in what was now called the "side garden," a lofty country-house-type name for what was in reality a strip of earth two feet by fifty feet, and unwound a ribbon of color from March through September: bearded irises, London pride, stock, bluebells, blood-red poppies, Canterbury bells, a small peach tree that rarely yielded more than a single peach, red-hot pokers, snapdragons, fragrant lilies of the valley, hollyhocks. No wonder he didn't appreciate the journeys of my various soccer, cricket, and tennis balls as they smacked off the fence and ran free, like the self-guided ball in Werner Herzog's *Enigma of Kasper Hauser*, to disturb the flowers.

Throughout his twenties and thirties, however, he was still vital and active. He loved to play tennis and take Sunday rambles in the English countryside, leave the choking city to which he was bound by family and employment and lose himself in the delights of bramble and thicket, rain-soaked meadows, profusions of wildflowers, and birds singing all the way through Windsor, Oxfordshire, and Gloucestershire. (This was a poor man's pastime. My Uncle Simey, my father's younger brother, used to take dates to the criminal courts at the Old Bailey to catch a free drama because he could not afford the price of a theater ticket.)

He met Doris (née Devorah) Shrier, my mother-to-be, in 1931. They were both members of a North London dramatic society. My mother had a starring role in whatever play they were performing, while my father was given only one line, or rather one word: "No." He muffed his cue and said it at the wrong time. Offstage, however, he played his part much better: he brought my mother flowers and chocolates and a leather-bound copy of *The Complete Plays of William Shakespeare* inscribed "To Juliet, from Romeo."

They married in 1932 and moved from their respective homes in Hackney and Dalston to Dollis Hill, which, with its tree lined streets and as yet half developed open fields, seemed bucolic in contrast to the places in which they had grown up. There they shared a two family house on the north side of Gladstone Park with my mother's older sister Rene and her husband Joe. Shortly before my brother Geoffrey was born in February 1934 my parents moved to Helena Road on the other side of the park. My father's steady white-collar job enabled him to provide a good life for his family in tough economic times. My parents were even able to hire a maid, Jenny, a woman who, incongruously in their tiny semi-detached house, wore a uniform and was summoned from one room to another by a bell that my mother rang, even though her voice could easily have carried the distance. For years my mother spoke wistfully of Jenny, as if we were one of Jane Austen's formerly landed families in decline. When the time came there was enough money to send Geoffrey to a private elementary school, Westcroft. Lew and Doris socialized with friends and relatives, went to the movies, attended synagogue on the Sabbath and all the festivals, played tennis, listened to the radio, read, danced, and played with their son in their well-tended garden, or in the park. They did not own a car.

The war brought an end to the halcyon years of my parents' marriage. My father, disqualified from service on account of his heart condition, worked at the United Synagogue by day and volunteered by night as a firewatcher (like Graham Greene) on the roof of his office building in Woburn Square. It was a dangerous job. When the bombs fell, my father spotted the explosions, then called in the site of the ensuing incendiaries. His companion on the roof of Woburn House was the young rabbi from Dollis Hill synagogue, Harry Rabinowitz, a Polish refugee and the descendant of an illustrious rabbinical family. My mother always claimed that the rabbi cowered behind the chimney pots while my father courageously stood his ground. My father neither confirmed nor denied her account. I liked to hear the story repeated. After all, I had a lost a tennis ball to David Rabinowitz; his family clearly couldn't be relied upon to do the right thing.

Geoffrey, five years old when the war began, was evacuated to the countryside during the Blitz and spent several months in Bedford before my mother went to join him. While they were gone, my father, from his desk in Woburn house, managed the quotidian wartime lives of London's Jews, for example securing kosher food for air raid shelters in Jewish neighborhoods. To pass his lonely nights at home he began to write an autobiographical novel. I have the manuscript. The early scenes in the chapter "Tenement Life" describe the protagonist's childhood in

Whitechapel: a courtyard with snow a foot deep, a large mongrel dog that sends four-year-old "John" scampering in panic toward his own "little doll's house," and this:

a late-night journey in a hansom cab with the driver in his seat up on top and the burnishing lights of the street gas lamps; a very small room with a spiral staircase leading to a diminutive upper room where there was a bed and a small table: here to delight me my father had brought some day-old chicks and fascinated I watched them picking away at their oatmeal; then there was the occasion when I ran home eagerly from school—class photograph clenched tightly in my little fists, and there barring the way to the courtyard was the publican's pet goat. I was afraid and ran. The goat ran after me—its horns perilously near the seat of my trousers. In an effort to reach safety I rushed forward wildly and in doing so slipped and then fell sprawling in the mud—but my photograph was still safe and I took it home with a tear-stained face to show to mother.

John grows up to meet Sally (my mother), and the narrative gets very Noël Coward, with lots of wit and repartee. Neither John nor Sally appears to be Jewish, which probably says more about my father's sense of the English market for novels at the time than any desire on his part to erase what was probably the salient fact of his life.

After only a few weeks in Bedford, my mother decided to bring Geoffrey back to London. She missed both the city and her home, and the worst of the bombing appeared to be over. For the duration of the war they sat out air raids in a closet under the stairs or in a neighbor's shelter.

In the summer of 1942 my mother was pregnant with her second child. David Maurice Wilson (the middle name after her father Morris) was born in March 1943 and, tragically, died a little more than two months later on June 1ˢᵗ 1943. The baby had picked up an infection in the hospital and didn't recover. My father never spoke about David, and my mother almost never did. It was years before I learned that he was buried nearby in Willesden cemetery. We never visited the grave, and we did not light a yahrzeit candle on the anniversary of his death. There can be no rules that govern mourning for the death of a child. I don't know how my parents suffered; I only know that they did.

Dr. Brostoff, my mother's GP, urged her to get pregnant again as soon as she could—this much she liked to repeat, as if it was justification (although none was required) as well as advice, and on June 9, 1944 she gave birth to my brother Stephen.

A few months earlier, on the night before Geoffrey's tenth birthday, the Luftwaffe and German Rocketeers had tried once more to return London to its primordial state and sink the city's buildings back into the muddy banks of the Thames. A stray V2 landed near our house and blew its roof off. My mother's friend Mrs. Borin had collected hard-to-come-by eggs in order to bake a cake for my brother. She had delivered the cake early on February 18, but when, on the morning after the raid, my mother came out of the shelter and into her newly exposed kitchen, our roof was not the only damage to be assessed: several pieces of shrapnel were lodged in the cake. To this day Geoffrey does not like to celebrate his birthday.

*   *   *

My mother was born in the London Hospital on August 20,

22

1909, and took shelter there as a child during WWI, along with her parents and four siblings, when the Zeppelins ballooned over London and dropped their deadly cargo. She grew up in a modest home above her father's bakery at 129 Shacklewell Lane, Dalston ("Shacklewell" because there had once been a prison at the end of that street). Her parents (like my father's) spoke Yiddish. By the time I knew her, my mother liked to pretend that she could barely speak or understand Yiddish. She regarded the language of her immigrant parents as a threat both to her English credentials and her bourgeois aspirations. Yiddish meant London's East End, impoverished lives, a lack of cultural refinement, perhaps even laziness. My grandfather Wolf, on my father's side, who was separated from my grandmother, and for reasons unknown to me more or less severed from the family, never learned to speak English at all; in the years that she was in contact with him, my mother despised him for his lack of effort. Nevertheless, her sentences were spiced with Yiddish words and phrases, and when I took her to see the movie *Hester Street*, she laughed a split second before the subtitles appeared. Jews, Kafka told a different theater audience, "I want to tell you, ladies and gentlemen, how very much more Yiddish you understand than you think you do."

My mother was not at all ashamed of being Jewish, but as she once told me, she "wanted to be very English." When she and her older sister began to go to school, they changed their own names from Devorah and Rachel to Doris and Rene because "it made life easier." Their older brother went from Lazarus to Leslie, but the switch couldn't prevent him from being denied a scholarship to the locally prestigious Cowper Street School on the grounds that his father, a Galician citizen of the Austro-Hungarian Empire, was an enemy alien. My mother's other two

23

siblings, Lena and Harold, began life with what my mother called their "correct names" already in place. My grandparents had apparently given up on the Hebrew Bible as a baby's name book in the process of becoming "Anglicized"; as a result, my mother proudly affirmed, "By 1924 we all had these nice English names."

The 1920s were probably the happiest decade of my mother's life. She was vivacious, flirty, accomplished, pretty, and courted by many young men. She played tennis at Lensbury on well-tended grounds owned by Shell-Mex, her brother-in-law Simey's, and later her brother Harold's, employers. I have the photographs: the men in long white trousers, the women, my mother included, in short flapper dresses, with white headbands in their bobbed hair. In these pictures, the young Anglo-Jewish players appear appropriately carefree and Arcadian, indistinguishable from their gentile counterparts.

My mother and her set, almost none of whom went to university—the women worked as shorthand typists, the men in civil service or the professions—loved English high style and culture with a passion. My Aunt Lena, whose acquired accent was my mother's fake upper-class telephone voice pitched to the edge of absurdity, read only the classics, studied opera and ballet, and took art appreciation classes. From an early age, my mother and her sisters decided to adopt as many of the external trappings of upper-middle-class English life as possible. One can see why: the English-English at play after the First World War appeared to be having a jolly good time, even when they weren't. They were children of the sun, bathed in the glow of that fiery ball not yet setting on the British Empire. However, for the Jews of Dalston and Stamford Hill, who had limited funds at their disposal, it must have been an enormous effort to maintain a veneer of class, and it must have been deeply frustrating to know that the club they wished to join occasionally tolerated but hardly encouraged Jewish membership.

The boyfriends who preceded my father in the Roaring Twenties (my mother, as she was quite willing to demonstrate, could dance a mean Charleston) were, as she frequently reminded us, high-level suitors: Gerry Barwell went on to become a doctor and Sammy Costa a radio celebrity. My mother always insinuated that my father was *not* the great love of her life, but the man she dated only at the behest of the one who was—her father. My grandfather had told her that my father was *bekovet*, which can be roughly translated as "honorable."

* * *

In the 1950s and early 1960s, first in order to supplement my father's income from the United Synagogue, and then to replace his income entirely when illness forced his early retirement, my mother worked as a secretary for two small firms: Drinkwaters, a refuse disposal company in Willesden, and then Davis Estates, a real estate office on Kilburn High Road.

In order to get to Davis Estates, my mother walked ten minutes to a tube station, took a ten-minute train ride, and then walked another five minutes to the office. Instead of taking a lunch hour for herself, she would come home, make me something to eat on my return from elementary school—like all Jewish boys, I was permitted to go home for lunch as my school did not provide kosher food—and then return to the office. As you can calculate, she spent fifty minutes traveling to spend ten minutes with me in order to ensure that I got my cheese on toast or omelet. Sometimes she would be in a rage when I got home, for the simple reason that I had chosen to stay at school to play soccer for most of the lunch hour rather than head home to eat, and by the time I arrived she was already late for her afternoon's work. There was a reason for my selfishness: lunch was the only time of the day when we were allowed to play with a properly sized soccer ball, as opposed to a tennis ball. Who could resist?

In Saul Bellow's novel *Herzog*, the eponymous hero recalls a revealing moment from his childhood. We are in Montreal on a cold winter's night, and as darkness falls Moses Herzog's mother pulls him on a sled through icy streets. Young Moses knows he is too big to be dragged this way by his mother, whose strength is ebbing through illness and hardship, but he never objects to the ride. An "old baba" stops Mrs. Herzog and admonishes her: "Why are you pulling him, daughter! ... Daughter, don't sacrifice your strength to children." Moses will not get off the sled. Looking back, grown-up Herzog thinks, "I pretended not to understand. One of life's hardest jobs, to make a quick understanding slow." Like Moses Herzog, I understood very well what it cost my mother to keep me happy, and like him I too remained silent.

* * *

In the late summer of 1960, when I was ten, my friend Stephen Levinson's father kindly offered to take me to a preseason friendly between First Division Tottenham Hotspur's first team (The Whites) and their reserves (The Blues). My mother approved the trip even though the game was on a Saturday and I should really have been in synagogue with my father. Her first employment as a sixteen-year-old fresh out of Pitman's secretarial school had been in an office on Tottenham's Seven Sisters Road, where she worked for the Africa Canning and Packing Corporation. I think she held some vestigial nostalgia for the neighborhood, or perhaps more accurately for herself as she was then in that neighborhood—young, excited, free—but she would never have admitted as much to me.

We drove in Mr. Levinson's Ford Zephyr through working-class precincts with terraced houses and prefabs and parked near White Hart Lane, home to the mighty Spurs. For an irrelevant game like this there were not many spectators, which was a boon to a first-time fan like myself. We stood on a lower terrace and I could hear the players shouting directions and demands at one another. At one point, the great Scottish hard-man halfback Dave Mackay launched a ferocious left-footed shot from the edge of the penalty area past the outstretched arms of reserve goalkeeper John Hollowbread and into the net. Mackay turned, smiled (this was preseason), and shrugged: child's play. Back, back into the car. I fell asleep and when I awoke, like Bottom in *A Midsummer Night's Dream*, I had been translated. The magic had worked. I was Tottenham.

Until the mid-1960s, soccer in England was by and large a sport played by working-class men for working-class spectators. To my parents, soccer was anathema, a synecdoche for the difficult penny-pinching lives they had left behind in East and North London. "Your father was so poor," his cousin Regina told me once, "that his family called the rats the *machatonim*"—a Yiddish word with no equivalent in any other language that refers to the parents of the boy/girl that your daughter or son has married.

As Jewish children with aspirations, my parents never imagined themselves, even at their families' direst economic moments, to be "working class," yet the bitterness and hardship of early twentieth-century working-class life, if not the pleasures and humor of its close-knit culture, had certainly been known to them both. My father had worked in his early teens after school as a presser in a sweatshop, an experience that turned him into a lifelong master with the iron (his creases were perfect) but otherwise left no happy memories. My mother had listened as her mother explained how my grandfather's largesse with needy strangers had eaten away the profits of his bakery and, on more than one occasion, brought her family close to the abyss. Hence, to play and delight in soccer, as I did, was both risky and treacherous. It was as if by donning the yellow and green shirt of the Gladstone Park School soccer team I was implying that we should abandon our suburban home in Dollis Hill and embrace instead the cluster of misery and ragtag squalor that was attached to the terraced house on Christian Street in Whitechapel, where my father had been born.

Like my mother and my two older brothers, my father had no interest in soccer whatsoever, and to make matters worse most of the competitive games that I started, for my school and for my club, took place in Gladstone Park. The park's official soccer fields, marked and with goals, could only be reached by traversing a railway footbridge. It was not a steep incline to be sure, but by 1960, even gentle slopes were hard for my father to negotiate. His leaky heart valves brought him to a halt halfway up the hill, where he would pause for breath. When I was very young he hid his condition from me by pretending that he had merely stopped to admire the view from the bridge; a steam train puffing in from Cricklewood Junction, oak leaves swirling in the wind, sparrows darting, men planting vegetables on a nearby allotment. I believe this is why I love certain paintings, like Tziona Tagger's *The Train at Chelouche Bridge* and Leon Kossoff's *From Willesden Green Autumn*, that feature trains rushing through a landscape that is at once green yet urban.

As it happens, my father only saw me play once. It took him an age to get over the footbridge, and from my position facing downslope on the wing, I could monitor his progress as he slowly advanced, holding my mother's arm. By the time he arrived, it was almost halftime and he had missed both goals that I scored that game, which would end in a stirring 8–3 victory for North West London Jewish Boys Club U11 over Golders Green. As soon as the second half began, he and my mother turned for the short walk home, which was of course a long journey for him. His effort had been enormous, far greater, I now think, than my own as a dutiful suburban American parent who turned out year after year to coach or view every single minute of his children's exploits on the soccer field. I went because I could; he came although he couldn't.

After the game, my parents took me to visit friends of theirs, Polly and Harry Layward, for tea. Polly and Harry owned a furniture store, and they had done well. They lived at least two steps up from us, in a pleasant house in the desirable location of Hampstead Garden Suburb. My parents were fond of the Laywards, although my mother was clearly somewhat envious of their material success. At one point during the afternoon, Polly asked me what I wanted to be when I grew up. "A footballer," I replied.

The moment we were safely ensconced in our Ford Anglia for the drive home, my mother, in a fury, whipped round in the passenger seat and slapped me hard across the face. She began to scream: "A *footballer*! Why couldn't you have said 'a barrister' or something professional?" I wanted to say "Footballers are professional," but I couldn't get the words out. The electric shock and deep resonance of the slap had stunned me into silence. My father remained silent too, as was generally the case in situations like this. My mother's violent reaction reached all the way back to her childhood. My pre-adolescent yearning to play professional soccer for Tottenham Hotspur was, for my mother, like wanting to be flung across town in a powerful catapult and returned to Seven Sisters Road. The African Canning and Packing Corporation, where she had worked quite happily as a teenager, was, with its neighborhood ghosts now threatening me, transformed into her own personal heart of darkness. She hadn't got herself shunted forty-five minutes down the District line from Dalston to Willesden Junction in 1931 for me to fall back among the plebs thirty years later. "I want to be a footballer"— why didn't I just say I wanted to be a working-class Christian? My mother's rage was large as the sinkhole she knew I would fall into unless I mended my ways.

Perhaps because they felt they had to compensate me for their poor attendance at my games, or perhaps because my father felt bad about the slap, my parents bought me a leather soccer ball for my tenth birthday. This was an extravagant gift for them, as it cost five pounds. The ball was of the medieval variety in that it had laces and required the application of Dubbin, an emollient that soldiers sometimes used on their army boots. It might have been a head kicked from village to village. On the day of my birthday, I dribbled the brand-new ball through Gladstone Park to Cricklewood Branch library, where I had to return some excellent adventure or schoolboy books, probably *Bunter Does His Best*, *William and the Outlaws* or *Journey to the Center of the Earth*. I had the books under my arm and the ball at my feet. I dribbled round the entire Spanish defense, which had spread out all over the park, and cracked one in for England on arrival at the library's cobblestone courtyard. I went in holding the ball and the books and was immediately admonished by the elderly librarian Mrs. Hopkins to "leave that muddy ball outside." I dropped the books on her desk, exited with the ball, and placed it in a small concrete dip at the foot of a drainpipe. Back in, stamp stamp stamp. No time to look for new books. Back out. No ball!! This was undoubtedly the worst day of my life so far.

My parents could not afford to replace the leather soccer ball, and when they told me this, it may well have been the first time I realized that our family did not have very much money. However, I was not left entirely in the lurch. Dad came home from work the next day with a ten-shilling white plastic nippled Frido ball, a substitute I just had to swallow and be grateful for if I wasn't to be a spoiled brat. The first street game with the Frido ball, Steven Levinson smashed it through the front window of our next-door neighbors, the Heritages. The Heritages were one of only two gentile families on our street, so everybody had to be very nice to them. The previous summer I had hit a cricket ball through the Levinsons' kitchen window and Steven had taken the blame. Now it was my turn. It cost my parents almost as much to replace the Heritages' window as it would have to replace my leather soccer ball. When they got over it, my mother would sometimes sing to me the following popular ditty: "He's football crazy, he's football mad, that football it has taken away the little bit of sense he had."

Chapter 3

Kilburn Grammar, the North West London boy's school that I gained admittance to in 1961 after passing my Eleven-Plus exams, no longer exists. The buildings, sold in the late 1980s to the rock-star-turned-Islamist formerly known as Cat Stevens, now house another single-sex institution, the Islamia Girls School. Stevens, who after becoming Yusuf Islam would offer a substantial contribution to the price tag on Salman Rushdie's head, was popular in my new school for his song "I'm Gonna Get Me a Gun." Only one boy in the school was rumored actually to own "a shooter," but all felt a necessity for self-defense. This was first because we were, by and large, middle-class children being schooled in a working-class zone. And second, because more than half of us were Jews in an area not well known for its tolerance of our particular ethnic minority. Fights and beatings were commonplace, but had little of the romance that seems to be associated with the titan struggles recorded in the memoirs of city boys in America. Dread and fear frequently filled the air on journeys to and from school, and, apart from one or two notable exceptions, boys from Kilburn Grammar rarely gave as good as they got.

I sat alone at a single desk in my first classroom. I was still baf-
flingly ostracized by a rump of the same group of boys who had
spurned me in my last months at Gladstone Park Primary School,
but most of the offenders had gone on to other schools and my
isolation was cushioned by the presence of twenty or so new boys.

Directly across the street was the Brondesbury and Kilburn
High School for girls. There, a girl called Lesley Hornby, my
precise contemporary, would bud and bloom like a hidden flower
and emerge, quite splendidly, somewhere around age sixteen, as
Twiggy. In the early years, while we stood waiting for the No. 8
bus to take us back to Willesden or Neasden (Lesley's neighborhood) or Wembley, one of my classmates, Dave Wooley, a thug in
yearning without the muscle to back it up, used to throw halfpen-
nies at Lesley and cruelly urge her to "go and get a good meal."
This same Dave Wooley once composed a poem, the only one he
ever wrote, which was published in the school magazine. It was
the result of a flash of inspiration that had entered his untrained
mind while he was standing on the platform at Wembley Park
station waiting for the Bakerloo line tube that would bring him
to Kilburn. The poem began: "Silence, the glistening rails ..."
and continued in that arresting vein for several more lines. It was
an excellent poem, which only goes to show that even in a callous
lout there sometimes beats the lyric heart of a young John Keats.
It wasn't long before Lesley's boyfriend and manager Justin de
Villeneuve rescued her from the indignities of the bus stop and
picked her up in his car. He was an "older man," and we were
both jealous of and intimidated by his presence outside school.

Aside from the queue at the bus stop, the only opportunity to
meet girls from Brondesbury and Kilburn came at lunchtime if
you took the kosher meal and were thus permitted to leave the
school grounds between one and two o'clock. As a result, there

was a thriving black market in kosher meal tickets. New boys, like myself, were often strong-armed into handing over their tickets at a cut-price fee. The basement of nearby Brondesbury Park Synagogue was often crowded with the adherents of other faiths, there to flirt or rendezvous with members of the opposite sex.

The two schools were strictly divided. We were not even permitted to stage joint dramatic productions. When the students proposed, as we did every year, that girls be allowed to play the female roles in our annual assaults on Shakespeare, the response was always a curt reminder that in Shakespeare's time all the women's parts had been performed by men, and that Shakespeare himself had often played a girl.

My brother Stephen was Olivia in *Twelfth Night*, and when my turn came I played Katherine in *Henry V*. Mrs. Rosemary Chirgwin, the school secretary, applied facial makeup; she had once rouged and eyelined the dancers of the Royal Ballet. She managed to make us look credible and quite attractive. Before going onstage, every boy in the cast squeezed my padded bra for luck. I was twelve and my voice was breaking. In the dramatic fifth act, I gave myself submissively to the English king (a boy named Duke). He stood facing me so that his back was turned to the audience. I had been instructed to lay my arm over his shoulder and imply a kiss. The audience hooted and whistled.

If the presence of Twiggy makes the schools seem hip, touchstones of "swinging London," the impression needs to be corrected. Kilburn Grammar strove in a variety of ways to imitate the great British public (i.e., private) schools. We had "houses" named after boys who had been killed in the First World War; "fags," first-year boys indentured as slaves to those about to graduate; and worst of all, we played rugby instead of soccer. Rugby, as everyone said, was a "ruffian's game played by gentlemen," whereas soccer was the other way round.

Rugby may have been the official sport, but we played soccer at breaks, lunchtime, and after school, executing spectacular dribbles and crashing in goals on the sloping asphalt between the wooden fence and the concrete gym. At peak moments, six games, defined by age, would be in parallel progress every day. From September through May, you could witness an extraordinary phantom ballet in which the players in one game managed to ignore the inevitable intrusions of the other games as errant passes or rebounding shots sent six balls careening, as if in a pinball machine, around the playground. It has been reported that when the great Brazil teams practice they sometimes do so without a ball, conducting an imaginary match from kickoff to final whistle, tackling, passing, heading, leaping, running, and diving for shots in a simulated, perfectly choreographed soccer dance. On the playground of Kilburn Grammar, sometimes I felt that the ball was an irrelevance in just this way.

Anxious to secure their credentials as bona fide teachers in the great English tradition, the staff valiantly strove to enact a kinky disciplinary code. Mr. Moller used a leather strap; Mr. Connellor rammed a steel ruler down the back of a shirt or blazer and reverberated it against the back of the head; Mr. Owen hit with a cosh (a small billy-club) and a "kosher cosh," a softer, rubber version of the original that was used exclusively for whacking Jewish kids because their parents sometimes complained; others used cricket bats, gym slippers, or canes; some boys were made to stand for hours in wastepaper bins, and others had their heads beaten against gas taps in the physics laboratory. "I'm sorry, Wilson," a teacher once said to me in a conciliatory voice, "I didn't mean to make you bleed." The headmaster, Mr. D. F. Williams, nicknamed Lop because of the

way his head flopped permanently on his left shoulder, preferred a *frayed* cane. Sixth-form boys, "prefects," were licensed
to beat with a plimsoll. They exercised their authority over all
boys more than two years younger than they who spoke back,
ran in the corridors, or otherwise infringed upon the rules.

The Dotheboy Hall-style beatings and humiliations were
made worse by the fact that no one's heart was in it—not the
teachers' and not the students.' We were obliged to go through
the motions because they gestured toward success in a Britain
that was beginning to imitate a meritocracy and appeared to be
opening its doors wider to the middle class; but with the wrong
religion, wrong accents, and day-school heterosexuality in the
ascendance, our attempts to duplicate the deep structure of
upper-class public-school life, with its uncanny sado-masochism,
were doomed. We were soccer, not rugby, or at best somewhere
in between the two, no matter how you tried to spin it.

Aside from the quirky presence of the "kosher cosh," Jewish
boys were not singled out for special treatment, either for or
against, although several teachers liked to offer commentary on
Jewish activity in the school. Whoever controlled the morning
assembly frequently announced, by way of accompaniment to
the late entry of Jews who had been at their own prayers, "The
Jewish boys are making a lot of noise this morning." Significantly,
most Jewish boys, including myself, chose to forego Jewish prayers
(it was my father who had persuaded the headmaster that the
alternative should be offered) and instead attend the School (i.e.,
Christian) assembly, which featured a choir, the public theater of
teachers onstage, and more opportunities for fun and games. We
generally joined in the Lord's Prayer because it seemed ecumeni-
cal, but fell silent when it came time to praise the Holy Ghost.
The music teacher, Merlin-Smith, a beet-faced Welshman who

made us close our eyes as we listened to Wagner's "The Ride of the Valkyrie," then open them and write down "what we had been thinking," would oblige us to participate in hymns by reminding us of the psalmic roots of the Christian Psalter. "You Jewish boys, you wrote these 'ymns, you can sing 'em." The gym master, C. V. Williams, ex-military with a bald head and a booming voice, annually declared that "ninety percent of the boys who don't run in the cross-country are Jewish." The statement held no truth, but we would not have been unhappy if it had; in fact, the "Jewish boys" were proud of this imaginary statistic, as it confirmed our sense of our own bold resistance. The cross-country was a grueling, muddy, two-mile slog around Parliament Hill Fields which hardly anyone enjoyed and which was only marginally superior as an athletic event to the Swimming Gala, which took place at King Edward's outdoor pool in May when the water temperature was a bone-chilling forty-nine degrees. *No* Jewish boys participated in that competition. In fact, virtually no boys at all took part; with the exception of twenty or so fanatics, we all brought notes. My father always wrote that I was "indisposed," a lovely euphemism for "disinclined."

In our immured universe, the teachers played out their stiff-upper-lip Battle of Britain fantasies while we waited for the first Beatles single to come out. While we were waiting, Tottenham Hotspur soccer club did an extraordinary thing. Shortly before I entered Kilburn Grammar, they had become the first team in the twentieth century to do "The Double," that is, win both the League championship and the FA Cup in the same season. In May 1962, they followed up this achievement by winning the FA Cup again. I couldn't have been happier, and when the choir at the school assembly sang "Oh Jesus I have promised to love thee to the end," I joined in with gusto.

Chapter 4

The first time my father nearly died was shortly before my bar mitzvah in March 1963. I almost didn't get bar mitzvahed at all. Unbeknownst to my parents, I had been skipping Hebrew school for months preceding the event, not only on Sunday mornings but also the Tuesday and Thursday classes which ran from 4:30–6:00 p.m. I had filled the time, of course, with soccer. Unmonitored and unmoored, I stayed late in the gym at school playing indoor soccer with whoever else didn't want to go wherever they were supposed to be. Sometimes our English teacher, Mr. Bailey, joined us in the games. He was a spirited Yorkshireman fresh out of Oxford, and, as English teachers are supposed to, he transformed my life. I won't rehearse at length the Dead Poets Society devotion that he inspired, but it was certainly there, albeit in an unusual form, evolved not by elite children at a private school but by the confused and heady mix of working-class Christian and middle-class Jewish kids that made up the student population of Kilburn Grammar. John Bailey introduced us to D.H Lawrence's short stories and the First World War poets, and he loved Shakespeare. He came from a working class background and disdained softy silliness. He was tall and thin, wore Buddy

Holly glasses, shirts with thin ties and corduroy pants. In the manner of schoolboys everywhere I thought he was our senior by decades and in later years when we happily reconnected it was startling to discover that he was only ten years older than I was. In indoor soccer Mr. Bailey was a tiger: fast and skillful, aggressive in the tackle. He supported Sheffield Wednesday, a team from his home town with a century long tradition, a wonderful name (originally a cricket club, they had played their matches on Wednesdays) and, for a while in the early 1960's, the talent to match it. He was the first grown-up I knew who loved literature and soccer with equal fervor. I viewed this psychic arrangement as something both to emulate and to admire.

At around the time my friends were getting out of Hebrew classes, I took the number 8 bus down Willesden Lane, bought an iced bun from Grodzinski's, the kosher bakery, ran as fast as I could under the bridge over Park Avenue so I wouldn't get mugged, and arrived home at the expected hour.

On Sunday mornings I hung out in the park near the synagogue and looked for pickup games. One Sunday, I joined in with a bunch of "old" Jewish guys in their thirties and forties. On my right was the free-standing concrete hexagon of Dollis Hill Synagogue and its adjacent classrooms where I was supposed to be in attendance, and to my left, railway tracks guarded by an avenue of dappled plane trees and high white clouds. The "old" Jewish guys provided a running commentary on the game and I couldn't stop laughing. One of them, Lenny Bash, hopeless beyond repair at soccer, happened onto a ball that I had curled his way thirty yards from the right half position; it landed directly in his line of fire. All Lenny had to do was swing his foot. He executed like a pro from six feet out. The goalkeeper stood no chance. As the shot went in, Lenny turned to me and yelled,

"Dream pass of a lifetime!" Morris, the bespectacled authority figure who ran the game and whose side had just let in the goal, stared at me and said, "Aren't you supposed to be in cheder (Hebrew school)?" I just shrugged.

My truancy was discovered only when I took my bar mitzvah exam in Jewish history, religious knowledge, and the text of an allotted biblical portion, a test that, in the strict English manner, had to be passed before you could be called to the Torah. The room was two floors down from my father's office in the United Synagogue building in London's Woburn Square. The rabbi who administered the test could not fail me—my father's elevated administrative position assured at least that—but I didn't deserve to pass. I had no idea why Saul had slaughtered the Amalekites. It seemed pretty drastic.

I was packed off for private lessons with a local cantor, Reverend Taylor. He was a kind and patient man. He played the piano and I sang. It was a winter of extreme and bitter cold, but his house was cozy and warm. At the beginning of March, the doctors told my mother that my father had very little time left to live: weeks, not months. By the time of my bar mitzvah, on March 9, he did not have the breath to speak, and at the reception a week later he sat silent in a wing-tipped armchair while Uncle Simey read a speech that my father had written for the occasion. My mother appeared, if anything, more irritated than concerned. It was clear that (once again!) my father was ruining her day. Her younger brother Harold, whom she adored, and whom she had not seen for fifteen years, flew in from Cape Town for the event; he was seated in prime position at the long top table while my father, in his silence, was confined to the periphery next to my grandmother. I presented my mother with flowers and chocolates. I opened the dancing with her while the three-piece band played "True Love." People smoked and ate and wore great hats. And my father didn't die. Slowly his voice returned, his breathing improved: he would live for two more years.

* * *

That year, I was playing for the North West London U14 Jewish Boys Club, always on the wing; since then I have never been anywhere else, aside from a brief, inglorious stint as a goalie in college. The wing is a place of isolation, and I took to it when my father got sick.

Our soccer club could not afford kit for the team, so Derek Solomons, whose skinny son Brian was a reserve, kindly forked over some of the profits from his Shepherd's Bush record store, which was beginning to reap the benefits of Beatlemania, and bought us all blue-and-white-striped V-necked shirts and black shorts. Brian got promoted onto the first team and everyone was happy.

The North West London U14 Jewish Boys Club team held a secret close to its heart. A number of our team members' parents had begun their lives in Great Britain as refugees from Hitler's expanded Reich; at least one, I learned decades later, had arrived on the Kindertransport, and all had left behind relatives that were never to be seen or heard from again. There was an aura of the unspoken at our games, a silence and mystery whose presence could be felt, but which at the same time remained detached from our noisy schoolboy lives. The British-born parents seemed, although in my case the appearance was deceptive, to be a little more comfortable in their own skins. The foreign-born moms and dads rarely if ever came to matches, and when they did I sensed them as somehow lacking in the energy and confidence

41

of their Anglo-Jewish counterparts.

In London, only eighteen years after the war ended and a few hundred miles from where a sizeable number of every team members' relatives had been murdered in the camps, we played blissful, undisturbed Jewish soccer on Sundays under the auspices of the Association for Jewish Youth. The Sunday Observance Act prohibited "Christian" soccer on that day (the first Sunday soccer match in England was not played until 1974; in Ireland there is still a ban in place) and so, abandoned to encourage church-going in a country where hardly anyone went to church, the city's scrubby, shrunken, netless municipal fields, from Harrow to Hackney Marshes, were empty and free.

Jewish teams, of course, did not play on Saturdays, but in truth we were not entirely Jewish in our constituency. If our numbers were short, some fuzzy ruling appeared to allow each team to include an unofficial token gentile or two. Ours was Paul Vickery, a goalkeeper. However, before vital matches, opposing teams would often protest the appearance of the non-Jewish ringers, and a loose test to determine Jewishness was sometimes applied. Could the alleged gentile repeat in Hebrew the first line of the great Jewish prayer, the Shema? Paul Vickery had been well coached, and when the challenge came—at halftime in a tournament match against the despised Golders Green—he stood forward in all his gorgeous, turned-up, freckled-nose blondness, shook his Rod Stewart shag, and enunciated. The other team was not amused. "Pull his shorts down!" someone yelled. Our coach, Sam Rolnik, intervened. "What is this?" he said, "Nazi Germany?"

In Poland as a young man, Pope John Paul II, then Karol Wojtyłga, also played in goal for a Jewish team in his hometown of Wadowice. This was an act of both goodwill and comradeship, for as Jonathan Kwitny reports in his biography, *Man of the Century: The Life and Times of Pope John Paul II*, the cry of "Get the Jew" was not infrequently heard on the town's soccer field.

Club commitments aside, I continued to play in the pickup games in Gladstone Park, where, in addition to honing my soccer skills, I received instruction on how to become a socialist. John Barker, one of the boys who had been with our group more or less since the beginning, had arranged my lefty political baptism. He was two years older than most of us, handsome and charismatic, and already a serious politico. He urged on me George Orwell's *Keep the Aspidistra Flying*; I read the novel without fully absorbing it, I'm sure, but I got the drift.

I lost touch with John when I was in my mid-teens. When I saw him again he was on the front page of every newspaper in England. As a founding member of the eight-person anarchist student group the Angry Brigade, he had tried (and failed) to blow up the home of Employment Secretary Robert Carr, with a bomb planted in the minister's front yard. He and his friends had also planted another twenty-four bombs, all intended to damage property rather than people. A number of the bombs had gone off. No one was hurt, but the court wasn't quite attuned to this nuance, and John received a ten-year sentence. He duly served seven of them at Wormwood Scrubs prison before he was paroled.

John knew something about damage and desperation. Even though his father was a journalist, the Barker family still lived in the almost-very-poor part of Willesden, and when he went up to Cambridge he must have arrived with more than a smattering of what it meant to be a poor boy at a rich boys' university. He had a thunderous left-foot shot, superb dribbling skills, and he ran like the wind. His punitive sentence and subsequent incarceration convened a great loss for parks soccer.

* * *

In the long winter of 1964, my father had a nervous breakdown, possibly induced by side effects of the drugs he was taking for his heart, which included digitalis, product of that beautiful life-extending but poisonous flower, the foxglove. My brothers were both out of the house. Stephen, in his second year of medical school at the Royal Free Hospital, lived in "digs" while Geoffrey, who had already begun a successful career in real estate, was married and living in his own house. One freezing night, our pipes lagged with rags to prevent them from bursting, my father surged into my bedroom and dragged me out. He was screaming "Fire! Fire!" as he pulled me down the stairs and out into the empty street. His strength, so attenuated in the previous few years, was superhuman, his grip on my arm vice-like. I stood shivering in my pajamas. My father continued to scream. He saw flames, but there was no fire.

Neighbors began to open their windows and yell at him. My mother stood in her nightdress at the door to our house. She seemed torn between coming to fetch us from the road and calling for an ambulance. Then she disappeared, and through the curtains of our front room I saw her pick up the phone. Eventually both the police and an ambulance arrived. My father, whose hallucination had abated, sat silent in our kitchen. A detective in a heavy overcoat tried as best he could to take control of a situation that had already subsided. My father was put in the back of the ambulance and taken away. He did not speak again for many weeks, maybe months.

While my father was in the mental hospital, I lived alone with my mother. On Tuesdays and Thursdays after she came home from work, she and I took a bus to the hospital, a Victorian edifice of dirty cream corridors and squeaky floors, where we attended the meager visiting hours. It was dark when we set out, and darker still, it seemed to me, when we entered the large room with moth-eaten furniture and heavy brown drapes where my father sat waiting for us in striped pajamas and a dressing gown. My mother spoke to him, and I imagine that I did too, but he never replied. On the table in front of him, one of the nurses had placed the product of his labors in occupational therapy: a leather book cover with a torn strip for a bookmark.

It was around this time that I started going to soccer matches more frequently on my own. I had been traveling by myself to occasional midweek afternoon matches at Wembley since Halloween 1960 when, ten years old and wearing a white rosette, I had stood deliriously happy in the pouring rain with eighty thousand other fans while England rolled over a supposedly invincible Spain, featuring the great Alfred Di Stéfano, 4–2, but this was different. Because of my father's illness, there were no longer any restrictions on my Saturday activities. My mother had too much on her mind to worry about my desecrations of the Sabbath, and in any case, she was not really a religious woman, only an observant one.

The first Saturday match that I traveled to alone turned out to be a disaster. It was early December, and the game was also a first home appearance for Spurs' new acquisition, the skillful Scottish striker Alan Gilzean. I was excited to see him in action, but I didn't have a ticket, and the game, against Everton, was sold out. It had taken me close to two hours to reach the stadium, by tube and bus. On the bus back to Manor House station, two young thugs crept in behind me on the upper deck. I sat with my

TOTTENHAM HOTSPUR

FOOTBALL AND ATHLETIC COMPANY LIMITED

Chairman: FREDK. WALE   Vice-Chairman: S. A. WALE
Directors: C. F. COX, D. H. DEACOCK, A. RICHARDSON
Secretary: R. S. JARVIS   Manager: W. E. NICHOLSON   Medical Officer: Dr. A. E. TUGHAN

ALL RIGHTS RESERVED

PRICE THREEPENCE

Vol. 57   No. 23

Official Programme

SATURDAY, DEC. 19th, 1964

OUR VISITORS TODAY

EVERTON

AERIAL VIEW OF GROUND

eyes down, staring at the litter-strewn ridged floor of the upper deck. Any turn or flinch could have led to trouble.

When, in the evening, I arrived home weary and disappointed, I removed my blue anorak to discover that the word JEW had been written on the back with some kind of marker. My mother wasn't home. I hung up my coat in the closet under the stairs. I left it there all day Sunday, but when I went to get it on Monday morning, it was gone. My mother had taken it to the cleaners. The coat came back a few days later, its stark message expunged. My mother never said a word about it, and neither did I.

Eventually, after many weeks, my father came home. He sat in the kitchen without removing his coat or hat. He was full of shame and remorse. I believe my mother may have been partly responsible for the punitive attitude that he adopted toward himself; for many years she had been unable to stop herself from letting him know that his illness was making her life miserable. I think he saw his nervous breakdown as the straw that broke his wife's back. He did manage to hug me, and then he said to my mother, "I'm sorry, Doris." I wanted him to take that apology back, but he couldn't. I was at least happy that he could speak again.

He died a year later, in March 1965. He spent the last weeks of his life inside an oxygen tent at London's National Heart Hospital. A month earlier, the hospital had attempted its first valve replacement surgery on a man considerably younger than my father. The operation had failed and the young man died. The hospital authorities decided that my father was not a good candidate for the new surgery, and so he sat up in his plastic tent and waited for the end: breath without world, world without breath.

My mother insisted that I not attend the funeral. Perversely, and damagingly, she believed that at fifteen, I was too young for graveside mourning. Many of my school friends were in atten-dance, and they found my absence puzzling. In my family, it was not easy to take on my mother when she had determined upon a course of action, although we all did at some time or another, usually with consequences that bordered on hysteria. For many years it troubled me that I had acquiesced to or somehow colluded in my own absence from my father's funeral, as if I had been responsible for infantilizing myself. Whoever owned the responsibility, the result was the same: a mourning that had no end.

Chapter 5

The first game that I played after my father died was against the Stepney Jewish Lads' Club in London's East End. It was snowing, which was unusual for late March. We had to travel a long way. The game should have been postponed, but it wasn't. In the end, only nine of us showed up. In wintry inversion, the field was white and the marked lines rough earth where the snow had been scraped away. After a few minutes of play, our stud marks made the pitch look as if a herd of deer had crossed it on an Arctic night. Shouts and calls came from an enormous distance. By halftime we were already losing 8–0. None of us wanted to speak. Snow fell; our hands froze. Toward the end the score had advanced (or regressed) to 17–0. I shot from outside the area; the ball evaded the Stepney goalkeeper, but hit a defender who was standing on the line squarely in the gut. He doubled over. The referee, undoubtedly feeling sorry for us, allowed a goal. Stepney protested. The ref explained: "The ball crossed the line when Fatty over there sucked his stomach in." The snow fell in soft white flakes. The lines were invisible. Back on the bus, back on the train, all the transport delayed all the way home.

I was in a downward spiral, but this fact didn't register with anybody as an effect of my father's death, except to my older brother Geoffrey, who was extraordinarily kind to me. By the autumn of 1965 my grades were in decline, and I was firmly settled in the lower third of my class, right alongside some of Kilburn Grammar's most delinquent borderline sociopaths. Several of my teachers were ex-military men for whom the death of a parent was something you simply had to absorb and move past. Counselors did not exist. When I returned to school after the week of sitting shivah for my father most teachers responded as if a heavy flu bug had obliged me to miss classes. "Where is your note?" my form master, Mr. Fogwill, asked. Before I could answer, my friend Keith Jacobs raised his hand and announced, "His father died, Sir." "Oh, all right, Wilson," Fogwill said. "You can sit down."

My report card, punctuated with devastating comments like "Lazy and incompetent," was largely a litany of "Could do better." But somehow, I couldn't. In all areas, it seems, I was deeply frustrated. I had a girlfriend, Judy, who wouldn't let me do more than kiss her, and when I tried on recurring Saturday nights in her brightly lit kitchen to let my hands rove, she would call out for her dog, Sally, and that dutiful mongrel rushed in to begin an assault on my ankles. I persisted with this misery because it seemed like an inevitable outgrowth of my inner state.

At home, my mother was generally in a rage. At medical school Stephen had acquired a girlfriend, Kate, who wasn't Jewish, and my mother had no one on whom to vent her anger but me. She plunked down dinner on the kitchen table then turned her chair to stare into the distance as I began to eat. Then she would begin to wind up a narrative about my brother and what he was doing to her that inevitably ended in tears and, in case I should get any ideas of following in his footsteps, dire warnings. Later in the evening my mother tended to calm down, especially if we played Scrabble. We sat near the two bar electric fire and plucked the tiles from a white cloth drawstring bag that my father had made in occupational therapy during one of his hospitalizations. Around the top of the bag he had carefully inscribed obscure two letter words, like AI (a two footed South American sloth) and LI (a Chinese mile), that might help a player out in time of need. After the game was over my mother would say, "Alright, you've done your duty. You can go now."

I went out as much as I could, mostly to play soccer: a season remorseless in its dissatisfaction. By May 1966, I had failed seven of the eleven subject examinations, the O Levels, which determine whether or not a university will offer you a place dependent on your achievement in the A Levels to be taken two years hence. Needless to say, no one offered me anything. Instead I had to re-sit math with a teacher, Mr. Roscoe, who could not resist using me on a daily basis as an example of the lower depths to which his pupils could sink if they didn't watch out. "Do you want to be like Wilson?" he would ask in his West Country drawl. "Do you want to be here next year?"

One day I skipped math, took the tube to Wembley, and sneaked into the stadium tunnel. When I was younger my friends and I would go up in autumn to collected conkers under the chestnut trees that lined the perimeter road, then we'd find a way past the guards and onto the terraces. Once, we made it all the way to the royal box before we were chased out. Now I just stood in the tunnel and imagined how it would be to walk out onto the pitch. After a while, I headed back home, but I didn't want to arrive early and arouse my mother's suspicions, so I took a walk in Gladstone Park. There was blue smoke wafting from braziers on the allotments behind the railway lines. I walked toward it. A couple of resolute gardeners were at work on their patch, turning earth, weeding, tending to vegetables. I had a five-pack (the cheapest unit available) of Bachelor cigarettes in my pocket. My mother had discovered another pack while going through my coat pockets on a routine prisoner search only a few days earlier. "Lucky your father isn't alive to see this," she'd said. "He must be turning in his grave."

*　*　*

In June 1966, England hosted the World Cup. I went alone to the country's first game against Uruguay. It hadn't been hard to procure a ticket. The game was listless and dull, and ended in a 0–0 draw. For the next match, England's coach, Alf Ramsey, dropped my favorite player, the prolific and mercurial striker Jimmy Greaves of Tottenham, and replaced him with the pedestrian Roger Hunt. I felt betrayed, but without Greaves England started to win and no one wanted to argue with victory. England beat Argentina 1–0 in the quarterfinals, and after the game Ramsey, who didn't like the way the South Americans tackled, called them "animals." Then England disposed of Portugal 2–1 in the semis before moving on to face West Germany in the final.

On the day of the World Cup final, my brother Stephen came home. My mother usually behaved herself while he was around. She suspected, I think, that if she exploded he wouldn't return, so she saved the pyrotechnics until after he had left the house. At 3pm the three of us convened in front of the TV. I sat in what, until a year ago, had been my father's designated chair. For no other reason than to annoy me, Stephen supported West Germany in the final. Even my mother was appalled. Not a single person in the country, and with a special vehemence no Jewish person, was supporting West Germany. But my brother, improbably, cheered both their corners and goals. I tried as best I could to ignore him. When he had graduated from medical school Stephen pursued a career as a psychoanalyst.

England's "Wingless Wonders" won 4–2 after extra-time. The team's three great stars, Moore, Hurst, and Peters, all came from the same club, West Ham, a source of pride for my friend Billy Grossman, who supported them. Billy was at the final; his parents had got him a ticket. The rest of our local soccer fraternity, who were not so lucky, rushed to Gladstone Park to celebrate as soon as the game was over. There were no phone calls, no arrangements; each of us simply understood instinctively that was where we needed to be. On the old field with trees for goals near the Anson road entrance we were sixteen going on nine, re-enacting the goals from the final and running in a Dionysian frenzy all over the pitch. When I got home my brother had left and my mother was back in her favored role as eruptive Mrs. Joe from *Great Expectations*. She never let up.

* * *

Almost a year passed before I was dragged from the slough of despond. Her name was Pat, and she owned the high honor of being both a classmate of and friends with Twiggy. Like Twiggy, she was a willowy blonde. In the long, warm, light-filled evenings of the summer of 1967, I picked her up in my mother's pillar-box-red Austin Mini and drove out of London to the near countryside in Hertfordshire where, in semi-rural villages with neo-rustic pubs, we drank barley wine and staggered into kisses.

That summer, inspired undoubtedly by Pat, I was the fastest

Jewish runner under nineteen in England. When I tell people this, which isn't all that often, I generally add some kind of self-deprecating coda: "There were only three of us competing," something like that. Secretly, of course, I'm proud, although my memory of the event is bittersweet. When I crossed the line in the hundred-yards dash at the Association of Jewish Youth track finals in a blistering eleven seconds flat, I raised my arms and looked around to see if anyone I knew was watching. I saw no one: certainly no relatives (they weren't at the meet or, with the one exception already described, any other sporting event in which I ever participated), no friends, not even anyone from the North West London Jewish Boys Club that I was representing. Eventually, after a search, I found Billy Grossman at the far end of the stadium near the long jump pit. "I won," I said. "Well done, Wilczyk," he replied. Some of my friends liked to call me by the last name that had belonged to my grandfather in Poland. After some months, the AJY sent a medal to the club. Ten years later, when I moved to Israel, I left this medal along with my other collected soccer, cricket, and tennis awards at my brother Stephen's home in Oxford. Unfortunately, when he moved from one part of Oxford to another, my stuff got lost in the shuffle.

I was always a fast runner, and this was lucky for me. I once ran away from a kid in Gladstone Park who held a knife to my throat. He was very determined at the time to discover whether I was Jewish or not. He kept asking me, but my urge to flee was stronger than my urge to reply.

I think I really got interested in sprinting as a sporting vocation rather than as a method of escape when Dave Segal, an English Jew, won a bronze medal as part of Great Britain's 4 × 100 meters relay team at the 1960 Rome Olympics. Two years earlier he had brought home a silver medal from the European

54

Championship's 200 meters. In Rome, he was disqualified from that event after two false starts. Dave wore black rectangular glasses, nerdy then, but hip in present-day Brooklyn. He was the last English Jew to win any kind of medal at the Olympics.

After watching Dave Segal win the bronze, I'd go out and practice running halfway around my block. I'd start on the curve outside the Solomons' house, pass the homes that housed the various families who had arrived in our neighborhood as refugees from Nazi Germany, and return to the "English Jews" end of the street.

In June, toward the end of the school year, I won the Kilburn Grammar senior athletics competition, after achieving victories in the 100 and 220 yard sprints, second place in the long jump and 110 yard hurdles and third in the high jump. For decades the winner had his name inscribed on a silver trophy and a replica that he then got to keep. Unfortunately for me this was the summer that the English educational system underwent a radical change and Kilburn Grammar became Kilburn Senior High, a nicely democratic comprehensive school with no competitive entrance exam. In the general muddle of the change over the old honorifics were mostly dismissed or ignored. I was given the original cup for one day only and my name was never added to it. There was no replica. "You won the Victor Ludorum," my mother said, who always translated up when she could. I had to admire her effort, and it was kind of her, but without the laurel I didn't feel like a champion.

*   *   *

Pat wanted me to take her to see The Who at the Starlight Ballroom in Greenford. They were the pre-eminent Mod band (see *Quadrophenia*) who ended their shows by destroying their instruments onstage. I wanted to go but I couldn't. On Saturday nights the local Mods in the vicinity ate middle-class Jewish boys like me for supper, then spat their bones onto the blood-soaked pavement. For bravery I had only to look a few thousand miles east where those other Jews, who called themselves Israelis, had bashed and stashed their Arab neighbors in less than a week. Where were they when I needed them? In any case, I didn't need them. In the front seats of the Mini, outside her house, in the dark dip between two lampposts, Pat unzipped my fly, her skirt short as my breath.

Because of The Who, my school had its share of boys with sharp scooters, porkpie hats, and parkas. Pat's brother was a Mod, much to the disgust of her father. A whole other segment of the schoolboy population was already on the dark side of the moon. Pink Floyd rehearsed in a dilapidated hall on Salusbury Road, less than a hundred yards from Kilburn Grammar; the band's music ran up the street and we heard it as soundtrack background to lunchtime soccer as we criss-crossed the asphalt, working our elaborate patterns in search of the perfect goal. Ancient Kilburn with its cutting-edge bands, supermodels, and schoolgirls with designated op-art haircuts and soft-porn school uniforms: St. Trinian's hats, unbuttoned white blouses, short pleated skirts: the heart's playground.

Pat's father was a bus inspector on the 112 from Palmers Green to Edgware. He and Pat's mother, the power in the family, never treated me with anything except friendship and accommodation. The contrast with my own mother was striking. Doris located and tore up some photographs, headshots that I had of Pat, and left the scraps on the desk in my bedroom. Then she called both Pat and her mother and, on the rampage, warned them both to keep away from me. Somehow I survived this extraordinary embarrassment. When you are seventeen you want, above all, to be brave in your love. Moreover, Pat was a boy's dream before Dave Matthews ever had one, so while it was completely predictable when my mother launched her assault and banned Pat from my house, it was equally certain that, despite her best efforts to capsize my love life, I would not give it up. I was, my mother told me repeatedly, "worse than Stephen" because I knew what he had done to her. Moreover, and this was an interesting twist, Stephen was a medical student and everyone knew that scientists and doctors did not understand the human mind. They were technicians of the body and psychologically inept. As a sensitive reader of novels and poetry I should have understood how a son can break his mother's heart. Also, Kate was going to be a doctor; that didn't make her Jewish, but it brought a certain exemption and a plus. Pat, in contrast, was going to be what ... someone's secretary? I chose not to mention that this had been her own occupation for many years of her life. One night Doris made me a delicious dinner of meatballs and chips (her speciality) but at the moment when she was about to serve up the plate something snapped and she decided to throw it at me instead. Then she abandoned the kitchen and went to bed. There was nothing to be done.

All June and July I was in a heady state, thanks to sex, rock and roll, and a blonde from Neasden. The first time I ever ventured out on a Friday night, ignoring the injunction to keep the Sabbath holy, I went with Pat to a Chinese restaurant next door to the Everyman cinema in Hampstead. In order to make sure the evening would be properly unkosher, I ate sweet and sour pork before we went on to the movies in the West End. In Leicester Square it felt like Walpurgisnacht: the neon wash of air was charged with the Cossack crack and electric pop of Christians on the loose. When the pubs and cinemas emptied I knew the revelers on the street would begin to look for Jews to rape and murder, but I didn't care. When Pat pulled me by the hand under the dappled plane trees toward the Odeon, I blinked with stunned amazement, like Eurydice following Orpheus up into the open. The pocked, veined faces of summer drunks moved in and out of the trees like floating moons. I was free, or at least I thought I was.

Naked on Pat's bed, listening to Georgie Fame and the Blue Flames, was, I'm pretty sure, the first time I found something better than soccer to do with my free time. I spent most late afternoons in her bedroom, which overlooked sailboats tacking on the Welsh Harp, a chilly body of water not nearly as pretty as its name. "Tacking" was a word I had learned by reading Arthur Ransome's *Swallows and Amazons*. It was something rich kids did in their boats on summer vacations; first they went one way, then another. They had the freedom to change direction, and didn't necessarily go where the wind blew them.

In August I went to Nice for three weeks to take a French foreign language course for high school kids offered by the university there. I skipped the classes and spent almost every day at the beach. I lay my towel on the smooth stones, covered myself in Ambre Solaire and read *Anna Karenina*. I returned to England to discover that in my absence Stephen had married Kate. Neither Kate's parents (members of a church) nor my mother (of course) approved, and the families, with Geoffrey dragged unwillingly into the mix as a surrogate for my father, had even held a kind of summit meeting to try and figure out a way to sabotage the lovers' plans. Too late: they married in a registry office with only a few friends in attendance. Just for the record, they are still married.

Ah, home. What an education I received there in the days and months that followed: in the competing demands of passion and duty, the obligations the living owed to history and to the recent dead, who owed what to whom in a family and why. Tears, sobs, improvised heart attacks, imprecations, soliloquies that scaled dramatic heights, were all in my mother's repertoire. She started early and ended late. I heard her out (I had no choice) and then I left to go and see Pat, insult and invective heaped on my head as I departed and more waiting for me when I returned. Here I come, tiptoeing up the stairs at two a.m. and there is my mother in her blue nightgown glued to a banister at the top. Her grey hair is tousled, her face inflamed, her eyes wild. "Where have you been?" she screams, "With her? With that girl? Never, never, never, never, never!" As Lear on the heath she would have been magnificent. One night Geoffrey and his wife Marilyn took my mother and me to a new restaurant in Golders Green. While my mother was out of earshot I ordered a sublimely unkosher sea-food pizza. When the food arrived Doris immediately spotted a prawn, picked up the plate, and threw it in my face.

Chapter 6

A year later in the summer of 1968, I graduated from Kil-burn Grammar. I was eighteen. Every university to which I had applied rejected me. I awaited the results of my A Levels, certain of the failure that my teachers had assured me I deserved: the penalty for laziness, inattentiveness, truancy or, as I thought of it, love.

In July I got a job working on a building site in Holborn. The employment came courtesy of Edith Muller, mother of my first girlfriend Judy. Edith had a relative who supervised construction workers for Bovis and all of a sudden there I was as a chippie's (carpenter's) assistant working inside the elevator shaft of build-ing undergoing renovation. I held planks while my Jamaican superior (the chippie) drilled holes in them. On the first day he told me that if a plank moved while he was drilling he was going to kill me. The building site was a place of rare antics and low comedy. People would drop heavy items from high floors, yell "watch out" at the last moment and then laugh extravagantly. Lunchtime seating was segregated: West Indians at one table, Irish at another. I wasn't sure where Jews were supposed to go so I sat with a Sikh. He gave me a lot of advice about sex and had some strange ideas about vaginas which, according to him, were not universally north/south: Asian women's, he said, went west/east. After lunch we all trooped outside for five minutes to yell and whistle at female passers by. At the end of the day I took the tube home quite happy with the quality of my unsentimental education. Then, disaster: Billy Grossman's mother saw me walking past her house and decided that I "looked tired". She phoned Edith Muller who got in touch with her relative and told him to tell the foreman on site not to work me so hard. When I turned up the next day word had already got around. Everyone ignored me, I would learn no more about international vaginas.

To pass the time before confirmation of my inevitable academic failure, and to enjoy an age-appropriate adventure, I went in the company of two soccer friends from Willesden, Billy Grossman and Sam Cornberg, to be a volunteer worker on Kibbutz Lehavot Haviva near the town of Hadera in central Israel. I had made good money on the Bovis site and was able to cover my own airfare. On the kibbutz, of course, room and board was free. Until the previous year's Six-Day War I had known very little about Israel, but that astonishing week in June 1967 changed everything. *We* beat *them*. Case closed. Or at least, case altered. My mother was happy for me to visit the Jewish state although she warned me not to get any ideas about staying. She hoped I would meet a "nice Jewish girl" in Israel although preferably not an Israeli, and certainly not a dark-skinned Sephardic Israeli from Morocco or Yemen or somewhere awful like that. What I needed was a "nice, English Jewish girl" who, with any luck, I would find working alongside me in the kibbutz's groves and orchards. Pat meanwhile was on holiday in Devon with her parents and brothers. In my wallet I carried a thumbnail photograph of her, the only one that had managed to survive my mother's earlier assault on her image.

Despite, or perhaps because of, the eight years I had spent in Hebrew school, my Hebrew skills were laughable and they hardly improved on the kibbutz where English was the lingua franca for conversation among and with the volunteers. The members of Lehavot Haviva were an odd mix of older Czechs and younger Argentinians; this would resonate later as a salient fact when we played them in soccer. Camp numbers were visible on some of the arms of the Europeans. I worked mainly in "the cotton" and the *machsan tsinorot*, pipe workshop, fixing sprinklers and then moving pipes for irrigation purposes. Somewhere along the line I broke my glasses and all I had left were my prescription sun-glasses, so the nights were doubly dark to me.

The volunteer culture, as I would also learn in later years, was generic. Suffice to say that it frequently involved a guitar and very bad singing. Here's what I mainly remember. A young Eng-lishman called Nicholas referred to his well-endowed girlfriend Phyllis's bras as "tit-bags." I hated it when he used the expression because I was a neo-romantic. I haven't been able to get "tit-bags" out of my head for more than forty years. A handsome Arab worker with a pencil-thin moustache like Ronald Colman used to come to the swimming pool when we were all up there and the kibbutzniks were enjoying their siestas. He hit on the girls and sometimes he asked them if they wanted to go and make "fig-fig" with him in the fields. I don't know if any of them did. It was quite clear that the male kibbutzniks, even those who were married, were allowed to seduce the female volunteers. But male volunteers were like young tribesmen who hadn't passed their initiation rites. We lived together in huts, and all the Israeli women were off-limits. In any case none of us stood a chance. We were a bunch of wimpy Westerners up against the heroes of the Six-Day War. Not that I was much interested anyway, on account of Pat, with whom I exchanged long summer love-letters, but even if I had been, forget it.

As you might guess, no one's mind was on Zionism. Some of the Jewish volunteers got sentimental at certain times and excited at others—especially when we were bussed to see the rock band Kaveret. A number of kibbutzniks urged us to come and live in Israel. Almost all the volunteers swore that they would. I didn't. At the time I was tied up with Pat, and I wasn't at all averse to returning home. As it turned out, I was the only person in our expanded group who ever went back to live in Israel. A group of Czech students were also at Lehavot Haviva, courtesy of Prime Minister Dubcek's liberalizing reforms. In August the Russian tanks rolled in and turned the Prague spring into winter. Our Czechs were stranded. One of them, Tomas Kulka, never left Israel and became a philosophy professor at Hebrew University. Another volunteer, also named Tomas, wound up at London University studying Chinese.

On the night before we were due to depart, the English volunteers challenged the Argentine kibbutzniks to a game. It was to be a tense replay of the World Cup quarterfinal from two years earlier. We were all Jews, but when it came to soccer loyalty, somehow it was clear that country came first. We played under lights on an outdoor basketball court. I experienced a little difficulty because of my lost glasses. Moreover, I hadn't brushed my hair for several weeks, and, as I discovered when I went up to head the ball, there were several twigs in it. Despite this minor handicap we were a tight team, as four or five of us had played together in North West London before signing up as volunteers.

Night soccer, I would venture, is even better than night swimming: one's sense of speed is heightened and you feel much more like bringing out the full repertoire of party tricks: flicks, back-heels, glances, dummies. It's exhilarating. We won 4–3, and Bill Grossman dutifully recorded the result and the scorers in his notebook, as he had for every game we played together since we were ten. This is how I know that I scored two goals that night, my first on foreign soil.

* * *

As it happens, I did well in my A Level exams, and to everyone's surprise it looked as if I might get a university place after all, on the "clearing system," the safety valve that opens for late bloom-ers and allows them to replace hot candidates who have some-how screwed up. However, once again I was rejected, and the world of a nine-to-five job beckoned. Luckily Geoffrey, who had attended a real public (i.e. private) school, been an officer in the British army, and was already a successful businessman, con-trived to circumvent the system. He placed an advertisement in the Establishment newspaper of the day, the London *Times*, list-ing my grades and outlining my predicament. Within twenty-four hours I had two offers of interviews for places, and found one at the University of Nottingham.

Perhaps because I had secured my spot in this slightly unfair way and so felt fraudulent, or perhaps because the subject that I was admitted to study—medieval and modern history—held little interest for me at the time, or perhaps simply because it was 1968 and I was eighteen, I did almost no work whatsoever at Nottingham. I attended hardly any classes and sat for no exams.

England at the end of the sixties was both of and apart from the great revolution that swept Europe and America. Bill Clin-ton took up his Rhodes Scholarship in Oxford in 1968, a stirring

64

time almost everywhere except the British Isles, and an odd place for an American to have his political consciousness honed. Apart from eruptions on three or four campuses, what happened *politically* in England in 1968 was, basically, nothing. *Culturally*, however, the country was on a creative high. One of the curiosities of the European and American student upheavals is the fact that their background music came out of non-revolutionary England: anthems like the Stones' "Street Fighting Man," or The Who's "Won't Get Fooled Again."

The music, of course, ran off a drug current almost equal in power to the one wired through the United States. In his first year at Oxford, Bill Clinton lived at 46 Leckford Road, a house that was occupied the following year by Howard Marks, an undergraduate from Wales who ran a hefty marijuana and hashish business that by 1970 had gone international and by 1973 had escalated into a worldwide operation. Howard became the infamous "Mr. Nice," the title of both his autobiography and the film made about him starring Rhys Ifans. In early 1996, on assignment from *The New Yorker*'s Tina Brown, I went to Majorca to interview him at his home in La Villetta, to which he had returned on parole after serving seven years of a twenty-year sentence in the United States Penitentiary in Terre Haute, Indiana. Howard told me, between sets in a tennis match (in Terre Haute's "Club Fed," he had kept up his game by participating in frequent matches against some of Chicago's best gang leader athletes), that he had sold Bill Clinton the joints that the President-to-be hadn't inhaled. But who knows?

Why did England stay quiet in 1968? There are a few obvious answers: a Labour government was in power; British students were a privileged minority group whose education *and* spending money were financed by the government, and unlike their French counterparts, they didn't suffer the hardships of overcrowded classrooms and an intolerably rigid educational system; there was no draft, and, again unlike the French, no direct link to Vietnam; there was no student leadership, no charismatic figure equivalent to Daniel Cohn-Bendit in France or Rudi Dutschke in West Germany; in England it was impossible to cross class barriers and build a bridge between workers and students (as was briefly the case in France). For, while British students venerated workers, the workers themselves considered the students to be spoiled, advantaged, upper- and middle-class whiners. Add to all these some further factors: the lack of a revolutionary tradition (Cromwell really was an aberration), the insularity of the British and their ongoing suspicion of movements that arrive from the rest of Europe or the United States, the nation's collective unexcitable temperament—it becomes quite surprising that the brushfires at the London School of Economics, the University of Essex, and the Hornsey College of Art occurred at all.

At the University of Nottingham, a hundred miles or so from the radical epicenters listed above, nobody cared that the biggest student party of the twentieth century was in full swing. So, like the majority of the country, I too stayed quiet. I read Dostoyevsky and patronized Robin Hood-themed restaurants like The Maid Marian and drank in The Trip to Jerusalem, the oldest pub in England, where, in the fourteenth-century, crusaders had supposedly knocked back a few jugs of ale before setting off to murder and rape people who didn't want to be Christians. I was, I think, deeply lonely. Aside from reading, I didn't know too many routes out of loneliness, but one I could always fall back on was soccer.

I did, of course, play soccer, but not for the university team; I was nowhere near good enough for that. Instead, along with two guys from Newcastle who, like me, were hell-bent on getting themselves rusticated, I got involved in an endless series of pickup games on the green in front of Lincoln Hall, our dorm, and once in Sherwood Forest. It was the first time I had ever played what I considered to be "northern soccer." Nottingham isn't in the north of England, but if you come from London it is. Soccer "up north" is traditionally faster, tougher, better than the soccer played by those frail flowers in the south. As it turned out I didn't feel myself outclassed, but this was undoubtedly because while the individuals I played alongside and against all had northern accents, they were from middle-class homes just like mine.

In late August 1968, on my first trip up to scout the city of Nottingham after my acceptance at the university, I had gone to a game between Nottingham Forest and Leeds United. I was in the City Ground in a crowd of 31,000 when, an hour or so into the match, wisps of smoke appeared in the main stand. Suddenly there were flames and the spectators, myself included, spilled onto the pitch. The players, who did not quite realize what was going on, stood hands on hips, bewildered on the field. And there I was at last, accidentally in the dream world of soccer, rubbing shoulders with the gods, the great Scottish midfielder Jim Baxter, and all those superb bastards from Leeds: Bremner, Giles, Gray, and Jack Charlton. I stood in awe and rapture in the center circle of a bona fide professional First Division English soccer club. The flames licked the roof of the stand. I remained as long as I could, until the police and the club's stewards began to shepherd everyone out of the stadium. No one had been hurt, and everyone from the main stand escaped through the exits or onto the field.

I was still Tottenham, of course, but for one year in Nottingham after classes began, I hardly missed a single Forest home game. Once or twice I went with a friend, but mostly I was alone. I didn't understand, although it must certainly have been the case, that the City Ground was my home away from home.

The University of Nottingham owned a collection of erotic paintings by D. H. Lawrence, which I saw on one of the rare days that I ventured to class. While disappointing as both paintings and pornography, they provided a fitting backdrop to my other major pursuit while I was in residence: waiting for Pat to come up on weekends. She did so a few times and it was awkwardly great, but inevitably time, distance, the eros of her office life in London, my moral turpitude on campus, and the magnetic charms of one of her former boyfriends (whom she later married) combined to set us apart.

In May 1969, having failed to show up to any exams, I executed a preemptive strike and left the university before they could ask me to. I have to say that the authorities were very kind and understanding, as if my abject failure had been their fault and not mine.

Chapter 7

I didn't stay quiet for long. After a year working for Jones Lang Wootton, a firm of London surveyors (a job secured for me by Geoffrey—I was entirely adequate at holding the other end of a tape measure), I was admitted to the University of Essex, where there was certainly a party to attend if one so desired. I arrived to catch the tail end of it in the autumn of 1970.

I had a mythopoeic initiation. As I arrived and crossed the main quadrangle toward a blue fountain, a naked student stepped from the swirling basin, like Aphrodite coming ashore, and stretched her arm out toward me. A long bloody gash ran from beneath her elbow almost down to her wrist. "Wanna lick this?" she asked. I declined, but I knew, happily, that when I passed this gatekeeper I would enter the netherworld that I had been looking for since leaving Kilburn Grammar.

Essex did not disappoint. The place had a surreal quality; the buildings looked like something out of Jean-Luc Godard's *Alphaville*, but set in the pastoral surroundings of Wivenhoe Park, which John Constable had once found beguiling enough to paint. Oddly isolated, like the whole of East Anglia, despite its physical proximity to London, and with a student body of fewer than two thousand, the university was an unlikely site for apocalyptic she-nanigans. Nevertheless, for young radical politicos and prospective carnival revelers, Essex was the place to be.

In my freshman year, I lived on the top floor of what the now-defunct tabloid *News of the World* called a "Tower of Sin"—one of six high-rise dormitories that swayed when the wind blew hard and that, according to the newspaper, were home to every kind of vice and depravity. There, Tim Piggot, who occupied the room next to mine and played the Internationale sung in Chinese every morning on his record player, (he was both a Maoist and a member of the Spartacus League) passed me a fat hash and tobacco spliff with a cardboard filter, and after considerable inhalation, I threw up. I did better with the marijuana joints provided by two gay students on my floor, Robbie and Steve who, whenever I entered the communal kitchen area would say, "Here she comes."

At registration I met Eleni Christopulos, who looked the way I had imagined Anna Karenina to appear when I first came across her in Tolstoy's pages on the beach in Nice; that is, a person with long dark hair with some curls, thick black eyebrows, deep set dark eyes, and a very pretty face. Eleni's family was from Cyprus, not Russia, and I have no idea now if Tolstoy's description in any way approximates mine. I could look up his depiction of course, but somehow I don't want to. I tried everything I could to get Eleni to be my girlfriend but she already had a guy in London. Somewhere around November, however, she decided to give me a shot. After that we were together for seven years.

Essex had a reputation. In the spring of 1968, the university erupted over the campus visit of a guest lecturer, a chemist from Porton Down, a government facility that at the time was busy making poisons for use in Vietnam. Faculty and students had united to shut down the university and hold a series of U.S.-style teach-ins.

Two years later those of us who followed felt pressure to live up to the achievements of our predecessors. We staged sit-ins to protest the curriculum: the whole of the third trimester my freshman year was indeed devoted to a course entitled Revolution— study of the politics, philosophy, literature, and art of the Chinese, Cuban, and Russian revolutions—but we all knew this was an attempt to placate us, a fine example of what Herbert Marcuse called "repressive tolerance." We blockaded the points of delivery to the food halls to protest rising cafeteria prices. We also staged a "smoke-in" to challenge the university's post-trial suspension of two students who had been arrested and fined for possession of several slabs of hashish.

Police and the fire brigade were frequent visitors to the campus. During the "smoke-in" a bonfire, fuelled by trees uprooted from the vice-chancellor's garden, was set in the main quad, right above a gas main, as it turned out. The local firemen arrived in the nick of time, only to be met with violence and abuse: a student in a wheelchair with powerfully strong forearms briefly wrested a hose from a fireman's hands and drenched his would-be saviors before the fireman could regroup. Nobody knew, of course, about the potential disaster. I watched the battle from outside the cafeteria in the quad slightly horrified by this assault on an authority that I was certain didn't warrant any animus. I stood near a student named Gandalfi who everyone knew had damaged the decision-making part of his brain with too much LSD. Gandalfi kept entering through the cafeteria door, only to come out a second or two later. When the potential scope of the disaster on the quad that had been averted became apparent the students should have apologized to the fire brigade, and thanked them, but no one did. Later that week Raffi Halberstadt, a bright, well-read American student domiciled in the UK, was arrested for trying to rob the campus bank after putting LSD in a milk bottle that the bank's employees used to top up their tea. Raffi's plan was ingenious but doomed: in his distorted mind tripping clerks would hand over their cash like free candy, but instead they called the police.

*　*　*

The fall of 1970, coincident with my relaunch as an undergraduate, an arresting personality arrived on campus: Robert Lowell. Lowell's three-year tenure at Essex now strikes me as curious but oddly appropriate. Lowell had turned down an offer from Oxford on the grounds of perceptible and foreseeable dullness, and had chosen Essex instead. What he wanted, it seemed, was to lend his own manic energies to the party already in progress. My tutor and later close friend, Dudley Young, who put Lowell up (and put up with Lowell) on his three or four midweek nights in Wivenhoe, captured (in a 1982 issue of the *P.N Review*) the impact of his arrival: "He was the large and lethal Carnival King, the Candlemas Bear come to release us from common prose; sublime, sexy, and frequently mad." However, while the English faculty, in general, bent the knee before the master, Lowell was regarded with suspicion by the students (at least half of whom had never heard of him), who were typically uneasy with Americans, who, unless they presented themselves in hippie garb, were assumed to be conservative whatever the strength of their antiwar credentials. If Lowell was going to be the Carnival King, he would have to get used to presiding over a very small audience. He had chosen to slum it, but he had a hard time staying out of the limelight.

In class, when he showed up, his boredom, so a friend told me, was apparent. He was merciless, ripping apart terrible poems, mumbling in almost indiscernible drawl. As soon as class was over he headed for the bar. He could hardly be blamed for his frustration. Poetry was under siege from the pop lyric, and Lowell was constantly asked to defend himself against Bob Dylan or Leonard Cohen. In Ian Hamilton's biography of Lowell, there's a damning description of these poetry classes, culled from a Lowell letter, as "rather retarded after Harvard." Elsewhere he describes the students as "inaudible and sluggish."

Lowell once wrote in a letter to Elizabeth Hardwick that Essex "looks like Brandeis, if Brandeis had been built on a fiftieth the money, and with no Jews." This strained image (perhaps he meant this kindly, but what does a university campus look like without Jews?) quite unintentionally gestures toward a truth: there is a point of comparison between the two schools, but not the one that Lowell meant. There were, of course, Jews at Essex, about twenty or thirty of us, and we had a convivial time there. One of the attractive side effects of the leftist challenge was a brief suspension (which seemed authentic at the time) of class, race, and religious animosities in the social realm. The feeling of commonality at Essex was strong enough (and unusual enough) to approximate the sense of security that Jewish students undoubtedly experience at Brandeis. Moreover, thanks to transatlantic cult heroes like Yippie leaders (and two of the Chicago Seven) Abbie Hoffman and Jerry Rubin, Jews were not only tolerated on our university campus; they were also—I think for the first time in English history—considered sexy. This wasn't true everywhere, as I discovered when I went to Oxford later, and the sexiness evaporated after the Yom Kippur War in October of 1973, but while I was at Essex, Jewish credentials were not a disadvantage. Only once during my three years there did I come across anything resembling the kind of knee-jerk anti-Semitism that was commonplace at Kilburn Grammar: an English professor, drunk at a party, brought a pan out of the kitchen where he had been frying up some pork sausages, held it under my nose, and asked me if I'd ever drunk pig's blood, and, if not, would I like to try? Even he, I think, actually meant no ill.

* * *

At the beginning of our second year, in October 1971, Eleni and I moved together into a tiny workman's cottage in the village of Wivenhoe near its estuary, close to the college campus, far from London and the disapproving glare of our respective widowed mothers. My mother, who remained a conscientious objector to interfaith relationships, had already banned Eleni from her home. "It's bad enough you have to go out with someone who isn't Jewish," she said, "But why did you have to pick a girl with Christ in her name." For her own part, Eleni's mother, dressed always in Greek Orthodox widow's black, was opposed to our living together on moral grounds, which had, I could see, a superior logic.

Our home featured no bathroom, a decidedly unpoetic outside toilet, and walls so thin that the neighbors' voices came through no softer than our own. The wife could be harsh "Pick, pick pick," we heard her yell at her husband as we sat down to eat, "You stick your finger so far up your nose that you're gonna pick your bloody guts out one of these days."

The rent for this luxurious accommodation was five pounds a week. The pub next door, The Station Inn, was appealingly shabby with a dart board, cribbage, piled crates of beer in a corner, and an eager clientele consisting of a mix of students and locals, some of whom were artists. Francis Bacon had once lived in Wivenhoe. Eleni generally had higher things on her mind than boozing, most particularly Dostoyevsky: the blue candle-wick counterpane on our bed was weighted down with novels and books by obscure (to me) Russian saints and philosophers, Tikhon of Zadonsk and Vladimir Solovyov among them. She fell asleep reading and woke, as I did, always at 4 a.m. when the local from Colchester jolted into the station over the street, like the train carrying Strelnikov in *Dr.Zhivago*, all lights, smoke, and screeches. That train did a lot for our sex life.

That year I played in goal for the first time in my life, for a student extramural team called Magic Moments. We were in a league that included a local police team, and before the games against them everyone on our team got stoned. Our player/man-ager, Ivor Dembina, presently a stand-up comedian on the Lon-don comedy club scene (the first of his cohort ever to perform at the House of Commons), owned a small tape recorder, and as we ran out onto the pitch he would push a button and Perry Como would begin to sing "Magic Moments." I don't recall the police team acting unnerved by this; they were far more frightened of our striker John Wolinski, who had a shot like a mule on steroids, but maybe it only appeared that way because of the dope.

I was okay in goal, apart from the fact that I wore glasses, which doesn't inspire confidence in one's defenders. Yet, despite my relative proficiency as a net-minder, I let in three goals against the local constabulary, but this disaster was not attributable to their attacking prowess. The goals, all my fault, came as a direct result of having spotted Eleni standing on the sideline with another guy, a graduate student named Allen with shoulder-length brown hair and a droopy moustache, recently returned from doing anthropological research in South America or

Africa—somewhere sexy. He definitely touched the back of her neck and, probably because my glasses were smeared with mud, I thought I saw them kissing. It took them a good ten minutes before they noticed who was playing in goal for Magic Moments and when they did they took off. I had not been entirely angelic myself in the previous months but Eleni was unaware of my infidelities and in any case they had taken place in London not Essex, so I convinced myself that they didn't really count.

One of my favorite books around this time was the whimsical and faintly surrealist French novel, *Froth on the Daydream*, by Boris Vian. All I can remember about it now is that its pages featured a character named Jean-Sol Partre. Before meeting Allen, Eleni had been plowing her way through Sartre's boring trilogy *The Roads to Freedom*, and also reading his novel *Nausea*, which perfectly described how I felt when I saw her on the sideline. Sartre, never a player as far as I know, once noted, "In football everything is complicated by the presence of the other team." I do like this, although it is not really very smart at all. It is only because Sartre said them that the words resonate. If I had offered his little aperçu to my teammates on Magic Moments, their responses would have been indifferent as nature itself to our existence on this planet.

I don't, by the way, advise playing stoned. As the Pittsburgh Pirates' pitcher Dock Ellis, Jr. said after he had thrown a no-hitter against the San Diego Padres while tripping on LSD in the summer of 1970 (he mistakenly thought one of his off days had been scheduled), "Sometimes the ball was very large and sometimes it was very small."

* * *

Vladimir Nabokov and Albert Camus were both goalkeepers.

Nabokov played for Trinity College Cambridge in the 1920s. He wrote persuasively of the charms of the position in his memoir, *Speak, Memory*:

I was crazy about goal keeping. In Russia and the Latin countries, that gallant art had been always surrounded with an aura of singular glamor. Aloof, solitary, impassive, the crack goalie is followed in the streets by entranced small boys. He vies with the matador and the flying ace as an object of thrilled adulation. His sweater, his peaked cap, his knee-guards, the gloves protruding from the hip-pocket of his shorts, set him apart from the rest of the team. He is the lone eagle, the man of mystery, the last defender.

Camus set up between the sticks for the junior representatives of a high quality team, Racing Universitaire Algérois. We could debate who was the better writer—I'd choose Nabokov, although the only book of Camus's I've read in French was *La Peste* (happily forced on me in high school), and it was bubonically great— but even if Camus was the weaker writer, he was clearly the superior goalie.

Camus once said, "All that I know about the morality and duty of man I learned from football." He probably figured this out over the course of several games, as goalkeepers have a lot of thinking time, especially when their team is crushing its opponents. With wingers it works the other way: they think when the team is losing. No one else has any time to think at all, and that is why both goalkeepers and wingers hold the potential to become writers and the others don't.

In February 1937, Nabokov delivered a lecture in Paris to honor the centenary of the death of the great Russian poet

Alexander Pushkin. Nabokov, then thirty-seven, was filling in for the intended speaker, a female Hungarian novelist, word of whose illness and cancellation had yet to trickle through the expatriate Hungarian population. Nabokov, in *Strong Opinions*, confesses his nervousness before the event but was, he writes, heartened by the sight of James Joyce sitting in the audience, "arms folded and glasses glinting, in the midst of the Hungarian football team."

In a later interview, Nabokov described the moment again: "There in the middle of the Hungarian soccer team sat Joyce—he was a rather small man, you know—and he sat there with his dark glasses on and his cane and paid perfect attention to my lecture."

The writer John Turnbull, to whose blog "The Global Game" I am indebted for bringing this anecdote my way, was led by it to ask himself a number of questions:

> Why was Nabokov certain that this was the Hungarian national team? Did they introduce themselves as such? Did he know them on sight? Were they wearing Hungarian kit? Or was this a soccer team, of unknown provenance, consisting in the main of Hungarians? A touring club side? An age-group team? Did they ask questions of Nabokov? Were they disappointed that the Hungarian novelist had not shown up? Had Nabokov (or Joyce) invited the footballers?

I doubt that we will ever know the answers. I imagine the surreal aspect of the combination of elements (Joyce, Hungarian soccer team, Pushkin, and Paris) appealed to Nabokov's mind; he loved crossword puzzles and moments of the unexpected. He might have been excited to see Joyce (after all, Nabokov was barely known at all in the English language literary world at this time) and surprised to find soccer players at the Pushkin commemoration. Hungary in 1937 had one of the very best teams in the world, and the next year advanced all the way to the World Cup final, where they lost 4–2 to Italy. In a time of great darkness—Stalin in Russia, Hitler in power, the world drowning in tyranny, Russian literary culture as Nabokov knew it dying out, and having recently completed his novel *Despair*—the fact that he even noticed the Hungarian soccer team is perhaps a tribute to his love for the game.

* * *

Sometime during my undergraduate years almost everybody I knew experienced what my discerning tutor Dudley Young called "a little local Altamont carnival's end." Altamont was a rock festival at which the Hell's Angels had stabbed a fan to death while the Rolling Stones played "Under My Thumb"—in other words, a party gone bad. One of Dudley's own parties had done so in my freshman year when the rump of the Angry Brigade (my old friend John Barker's group of anarchist students from Essex and Cambridge) had shown up and the evening had grown out of hand and then violent; items in Dudley's house had been smashed or stolen, and there were fights.

For students on the left, the moment of deepest disillusion and betrayal came during the nation-wide coalminer's strike in the winter of 1972. A large contingent of pickets from Yorkshire came down to set up at a storage depot where barges laden with Euro coal came in at Rowhedge port, not far from the university. Students from Essex reinforced the picket lines. They also moved in with friends, or slept on floors in hallways, in order to offer their rooms as temporary dormitories for the striking miners. There were frequent power cuts in our area, and the nighttime world, in pubs and on the university campus, was candlelit.

On the first night everything went well. There was a general feeling of mutual gratitude and bonhomie: the students gave up their beds and the miners (*real* workers!) bestowed their blessing. By the second night, however, the relationship had soured; a lot of the miners wanted the girls to stay on in the beds. They had heard all about Essex and read about it in the *News of the World*; they knew what went on: drugs and wild sex. They wanted a piece of the action. Some chivalrous boyfriends got punched in the face, and there was a lot of broken glass in the bars.

And then, to compound the damage, the National Union of Mineworkers, wary of their own reputation, carefully omitted mention in their press releases of the help they were receiving from the Essex students.

The curtain more or less came down on my own revels late one February night during the strike as I walked with a friend through one of the university's poorly lit car parks. We were returning from rehearsal for a production of John Arden's play *Serjeant Musgrave's Dance*, which I was directing. The play, set in 1879, focuses on three deserters from the British army who are holed up in a northern town in the grip of a coal strike and cut off from the surrounding area by winter snow. As if they'd read the script, two squaddies from the local army base appeared out of nowhere and jumped us. They had come down to the campus (so they explained in graphic terms as they went about their business) to do some indiscriminate beating-up in the aftermath of reading some anti-army, pro-IRA article in one of the university papers. They beat my friend Tim badly, smashed a contact lens into his eye and broke his nose. I got off with bruised ribs from a few well-aimed kicks. While we were driving to the hospital, Tim, slumped bleeding in the front seat, explained to me that the soldiers were not to blame for what they had done: they were simply working-class victims of an oppressive capitalist system. He was a Sociology major.

In early May of our third and final year Bob Marley and the Wailers came to campus. They were not the headliners at Essex's spring social events; it seems ridiculous now but that honor went to Captain Beefheart and his Magic Band. I had loved first ska (Rudy and the Rude Boys) and then reggae since Kilburn Grammar days and during my London work year I'd briefly had a great Jamaican girlfriend, Lorna McClaren. She loved the London theatre and after we'd been to see plays, Shaw's St. Joan at the Mermaid or something at the National Theater, she, along with her super-cool older sister Velma, took me to West Indian fetes in Harlesden where the rooms were so crowded that you couldn't move except in between your dance partner and someone else's. There was always rum punch on the table, Desmond Dekker singing the Israelites or Charles Wright and the hard funk of the 103rd St. Rhythm Band's "Express Yourself." The parties were unremittingly sexy. Once, Lorna and I took a trip into the countryside to visit Stephen and Kate, who were then living in Bury St. Edmunds and working as residents at a nearby hospital. We spent the night at their house then rose at dawn the next day; driving near Newmarket in a rosy mist we saw grooms exercising race horses, steam rising from animal's bodies, dew on the grass splattering from their hooves as they galloped down a long green meadow.

Less than a month prior to their arrival at Essex The Wailers album *Catch a Fire* had come out with its inventive Zippo lighter hinged sleeve, and on the night of the concert half the Essex students seemed to have the silver originals in their hands. The Wailers opened with "Concrete Jungle" which is what some people thought Essex looked like. Twenty-five years later, when my son Adam was sixteen, we went to Carnival in Kingston, Jamaica, and stayed in that lively and sometimes perilous city with an old friend from Kilburn Grammar, Kirk Phillips, who was also a friend of Lorna and Velma. Kirk took us to the Bob Marley Museum, there a mini-skirted guide described the statue of Bob at the entrance: "And here you see Bob," she said, "with his three favorite things: his guitar, his spliff, and his soccer ball." I have a postcard on my office door at work of Bob Marley in shorts and a singlet, juggling a soccer ball.

Chapter 8

I graduated from Essex in June 1973 with a first-class honors degree in English and European literature. Eleni and I had both managed to catch our desires by the tail and we were still very much together. My mother attended the graduation; it was the first time she had visited the university campus. Eleni's mother was also there, but we had decided to keep our respective parents apart. Eleni's mother, small, dark, and covert, with deepset, almond-shaped eyes and thick black eyebrows, had embraced her widowhood (Eleni's father had died three years before mine from lung cancer) much like my mother, and chosen a constrained and circumscribed life punctuated by social activities in the company of her children and grandchildren. She worked hard to sustain the small café in Fulham that she and Eleni lived above, and she worshipped regularly at her local Greek Orthodox church. She was a devout woman and a great cook.

One Christmas we took her to what we thought would be an utterly benign performance of *Robinson Crusoe* at London's Roundhouse theater. The performing company, Le Grand Magic Circus, was, it turned out, radically experimental. Man Friday was naked throughout, and at one point he swaggered into the audience and began to sit on people's heads. When Friday approached Eleni's mother with intent to squat, she reached into her handbag and retrieved her sewing scissors. Friday retreated. We had also brought along Eleni's young nephews, Jake and Dinos Chapman. They grew up to become "The Chapman Brothers" two of the most influential and successful members of the group known as YBAs (Young British Artists), their work steeped in sex and violence, nudity and castration—all our fault.

Once, when Eleni was driving along in London listening to a call-in show, she suddenly heard her mother's voice riding the airwaves and bewailing the fact that her young daughter was "living with a man." "How old is your daughter?" the host asked. "Twenty-two." The host began to laugh: Eleni always credited him with turning her mother onto side streets of tolerance and accommodation. My own mother was not so easily shifted.

* * *

I decided to apply to graduate school because I loved literature and because studying more of it seemed appealing. One of the Oxford colleges, St. Catherine's, was offering a postgraduate scholarship that included a year's study in the States. I didn't get that, but after my interview it was suggested that I take up a regular place, and I accepted. Before I could begin my studies, however, the Yom Kippur War broke out in the Middle East and, along with my friend David Friedentag, I volunteered to go and help out on a kibbutz. Oxford allowed me to defer for a trimester.

We arrived in Tel Aviv on the day that the largest tank battle since Stalingrad was taking place in the Sinai desert. As we exited the plane from London at Lod Airport, we could see giant C-21 transport planes parked on a distant area of the tarmac, bellies open and tanks rolling out like giant eggs on a conveyor. These armored vehicles were Richard Nixon's last-minute gift to the state of Israel, and they turned the war around.

I was sent to Kibbutz Kfar Azza, situated next to the Gaza Strip. There, the dearth of men led to job opportunities and after a week's training I was put in charge of a chicken hut. The cycle went as follows: feed, inoculate against Newcastle disease, immolate the dead (I learned what "pecking order" meant if you were a chicken), and then at the end of nine weeks, catch the fattened-up birds, stuff them in cages mounted on a truck, and dispatch them to market. Catching took place at night while the chickens were sleeping. Once I walked into a concrete feeder and lay on the ground covered in blood, shit, and feathers for about fifteen minutes before anyone noticed. Another time the truck tipped over right after we had finished loading it up; there were condemned chickens on the run for days—one even got into the dining hall where an obese man named Podro stomped it to death while everyone else ate lunch. I didn't show up to my last chicken-catch. I'd met a Swedish girl among the volunteers with whom I had been conducting conversations in our mutual bad French. My fellow workers, appalled by my lack of communal spirit, pulled me out of her bed at dawn and doused me with cold water.

Two weeks into the war, Ariel Sharon got his troops behind Egyptian lines and began to knock out SAM missile emplacements. At dawn one morning, bands of pink and orange spreading above the pines, the first captured missile of the war turned up on our doorstep for a breather on its way to Tel Aviv. Rumor had it that the Israeli army would quickly hand the SAM over to the Americans, who were desperate to get their hands on this piece of deadly and effective Soviet equipment. But for the moment, while its hungry and exhausted guardians wolfed down an early breakfast in the dining hall, it was ours. Soon enough ladders were set against the side of the trailer and Lilliputian figures clambered up to get a closer look at the weapon that had brought down plane after plane in the early days of the war.

After a month or so, the first reservists returned home. Kfar Azza was lucky, unlike its neighboring kibbutz, Nahal Oz, which had lost several young men. At a Friday night gathering of kibbutz members a tank commander described his experience after the lid of his tank had shut on his hand in the heat of battle.

One day I took a bus down into the Negev desert to visit David Friedentag, who had been sent south from Kfar Azza to run an onion patch on Kibbutz Tze'elim. I brought along a few bottles of Goldstar beer for the ride and that is probably why I mistakenly got off the bus several stops early. I found myself, Dante-like, at a crossroads in the middle of nowhere. There was a lot of sand, and tawny mountains in the distance. There was also a golden eagle sitting on a rock no more than thirty feet away from me. The bird was magnificent. He *owned* the place. Almost twenty years later, at a London hotel where I was staying on a journalistic assignment, the doorman greeted me, "Ah Mr. Wilson, there may be a message for you. If there is I'll bring it to your room." Ten minutes later there was a knock on my door. The doorman stood there in full regalia. "There is no message for you," he said. I thought of the eagle, whose communication had been identical.

I stayed at Kfar Azza for four months. I didn't see my kibbutznik friends again until 1977, when I returned to Israel, this time to Jerusalem, where they came singly to visit me. To my surprise they were like fish out of water, shy, a little embarrassed by their own heartiness, wary of the sophistication of the "big city." A serenely beautiful woman named Liora, with whom I had played tennis several times on the kibbutz, sat in a wicker chair in my apartment for an hour, almost speechless. She was the country wife in town for the day. Without tractor jokes or gossip about what had been going on behind the milk-white walls of the dairy, she was afraid she didn't have anything to say. Eventually, she left. Her mission was, as John Berryman remarked of a similar silent visit once paid to him by Delmore Schwartz, "obscure but real." True tractor story told to me by my workmate Petchka on Kibbutz Kfar Azza: in Hebrew the rear axle of a tractor, borrowing from the English, is called a "beckexcle." And what is the front axle called? The "frontbeckexcle."

Recently, quite out of the blue, Liora e-mailed me after a communication gap of thirty years. I told her what a great time I'd had playing tennis with her. "Oh I had to," she wrote, "I was in charge of looking after the volunteers."

Chapter 9

I returned to England in January of 1974 and began my studies at St. Catherine's. Eleni had stayed in Wivenhoe to pursue her M.Phil. The move from Essex to Oxford seemed interplanetary, far stranger than the one from Essex to Israel had been. For the first six months I felt as if, instead of advancing my education, I had screwed up so badly that invisible authorities had decided to send me back four years. Others have reported having experienced the same phenomenon. For upper-class public (i.e., private)-school boys and girls, Oxford was liberation from the ridiculous and arbitrary constraints of their earlier education, but for students who came straight from the big-city grammar schools or, like myself, arrived as post-graduates from other universities, the place was an elitist and paternalistic nightmare. Gardens were sequestered for fellows and other hierarchically separated individuals, gowns were required at most college meals, and *subfusc* (a costume of mortarboard, gown, and white bow tie) had to be worn during exams. For the Americans I knew (and it was Americans who were my closest friends there), the college rules and university dress code were stage directions, and they enjoyed being a part of the great British theater they had heard so much about. For me, they were unsubtle reminders of class, privilege, and place. There wasn't much one could say: to grouch about the setup or the system looked like ingratitude, naivety, and bad faith.

Although I had been admitted to pursue a thesis on twentieth-century American fiction, I was required to take and pass two somewhat unrelated courses before I could begin my research: Bibliography and English Hands. In Bibliography, I learned about papermaking, bookbinding, and printing presses, and the mathematical formulas for figuring out the correct pagination of Renaissance documents; in English Hands, I was taught to decipher eighth-century Carolingian and other handwritings.

My Bibliography professor, Dr. Fleeman, was a man with a concentrated Oxbridgian self-assurance and indifference to ridicule. In February I privately asked him to confirm the tentative date of the midterm exam because I had travel plans for a trip to Moscow and Leningrad. Eleni's M.Phil. at Essex included a thesis that she was writing on "Dostoyevsky and the Russian Orthodox Church," and I was to tag along on her research trip. The week after my request Fleeman swept into class in the kind of patented Edwardian fashion that some dons liked to affect and proclaimed to the thirty students, "The examination will be held on March 23rd, so Russia is okay." He didn't look at me when he spoke, and he left the rest of the class utterly nonplussed.

I did poorly in both Bibliography and English Hands. I couldn't quite figure out why. I wasn't noticeably stupider than my fellow classmates. True, I had not fared well on the other ancient manuscripts that I had once been required to translate, but they were written in Hebrew, not English, and I had been thirteen. I think, as on many other occasions at Oxford, I felt when I took on these medieval manuscripts that I was trespassing.

I was alienated by what I perceived to be foreign and extrinsic material.

* * *

On a bruised February afternoon not long after I had returned from Kibbutz Kfar Azza, I gave a paper in a study group at Merton College. I was still flush with the memory of riding high on "my own" tractor: the Jewish farm boy, tanned and muscled, a young man who had heard *real* sirens calling each to each, and spent a night in an underground air-raid shelter with the sad and beautiful wives of men at war. My subject was Bernard Malamud's novel *A New Life*. The title, at least, seemed appropriate. We sat around a long table in Merton's gorgeously authentic fourteenth-century library. As I read it, a new life for Malamud's Sy Levin turns out not to be the spacious freedom promised by the American Pacific Northwest, but responsible, resigned acceptance of limitation and restraint. Malamud's hero only achieves a breakthrough in the spirit when he accepts the yoke, not of the Torah, but of some unhappily modern equivalent of Mosaic law: thou shalt stick by thy troubled wife (in this case somebody else's), thy sick kids, thy miserable job. Why? Because thou canst. I embellished a version of this reading and the room was very quiet; dusky clouds gathered in the Larkinesque high windows, and then, in response to a question, I characterized Sy Levin as a schlemiel, and while it may not at all have been so, I sensed that this was a first for the oak-paneled room. *Schlemiel* circled the rafters, glanced off the stained glass, made its clumsy way around the long table. Sy Levin in America was trapped (but ultimately free), whereas I, for one delicious moment in the Christian atmospherics of England, and of Oxford in particular, was free (but

ultimately trapped). More than anything that arose in the ensuing discussion, it was this incongruity of language and setting
that impressed me: I was moved by a single word, I suppose in
the spirit of revenge, against the thugs around my neighborhood
and the teachers at Kilburn Grammar, the exclusiveness of
Oxford.

In 1974, there were somewhere between three and four hundred Jewish students (undergraduates and postgraduates) at
Oxford, about three percent of the total student population. In
a survey he conducted in 1970, the historian Bernard Wasserstein discovered, among other things, that while half the Jewish
students claimed to have experienced some manifestation of
anti-Semitism, "*not one,* when specifying its nature, mentioned
anything which had occurred in the university environment."
When I canvassed Jewish friends about their Oxford experiences
I got a similar response: almost everyone I spoke to said yes, they
had felt discomfort at Oxford, and yes, there was, of course, a
fair amount of anti-Semitism. But, as in Wasserstein's study,
hardly anyone could detail an incident. Or, if they did, the incidents were ambiguous, negligible, or the result of sensitivity to
semantic adjustments: a college warden who had introduced
himself in Hebrew; a guidance counselor whose first career suggestion had been a position at the *Jewish Chronicle*; being described
as "clever" rather than "intelligent."

I was hard put to explain this phenomenon, except in terms of
paranoia, until a woman who had been an undergraduate at St.
Hilda's exposed its roots for me. "It wasn't anything that actually
happened," she said. "It was the overwhelming Christianness of
the place. I felt as if I was there under false pretenses." The mood
or atmosphere that encircles Oxford, delightful for most students
and, in their imaginations, utterly secular and lyrical—a lambent

light over dreaming spires, horses grazing in Port Meadow, rain on the cobblestones down Logic Lane, a Brideshead Oxford—is underlain by other feelings for Jewish (and perhaps now Moslem) students. For us, arrival in the ancient seat of learning brings discovery of a different ambience, one created simply by the names of the trimesters—Hilary, Michaelmas, Trinity—or the aura, the Eliotic still point, that surrounds evensong at a college chapel. "It's all tea with muffins," my friend concluded. "It's never cheesecake."

For a few years after the Yom Kippur War, even the plaque on the house in St. Giles that designated the Centre for Postgraduate Hebrew Studies was missing. The brass rectangle was rumored to have been removed for security reasons, but its absence always seemed to me a symbolic self-effacement.

* * *

In March 1975, a couple of weeks after my twenty-fifth birthday, I accompanied Eleni to Russia. We had booked onto a group tour through Intourist, the Russian travel agency: it was not easy to move without an official guide in the Soviet Union. We planned a few days in Leningrad to be followed by a train journey to Moscow, where Eleni's supervisor, the eminent scholar and translator Angela Livingstone, who was already *in situ* working on a translation project, would meet us at our hotel and, we hoped, spirit us away from our minders.

I had imagined, somehow, that the flight from London would take seventeen hours; all the enigma wrapped in a pastry stuff had permeated my consciousness as distance. Australia, whose sports teams, singers and politics were a daily feature in British newspapers, seemed closer. Yet, a quick churn though cloudy winter skies and we were in Leningrad looking out from our hotel room toward the icy Neva and its moored memory of the Revolution, the battleship *Aurora*.

I had been looking forward to having sex in Russia (or anywhere really) but soon after our arrival Eleni developed a stomachache and sent me down to the bar to see if I could procure the Soviet equivalent of Coca Cola. She thought that a carbonated drink would settle her queasiness. We had been warned not to drink the local water, as the murky swamp on which Leningrad rested and back into which it was slowly sinking had somehow poisoned the wells, but Eleni's ailment seemed premature. She hadn't even brushed her teeth yet.

I had been anticipating a throwback atmosphere for the hotel, although just how far back I wasn't sure. Certainly the women at the bar (hookers most likely), peroxide blondes with beehive hairdos and exemplary mini-skirts, were predictably retro, but to my surprise the men, in expensive suits, shirts, ties and shoes, with well-groomed hair and bright, scrubbed faces, looked as if they had stepped out of a high end prime time American soap opera. The reason for this, it turned out, is that they *were* American. Before I even had time to buy the soda, I was bear hugged by a friendly giant, a tipsy Jack Nicklaus lookalike who offered to buy me a drink then let me know that he was part of a delegation of small town U.S. mayors who, puckishly, had decided to hold their annual convention in the Communist stronghold. "Comrade," he said, "any time you want to visit Manhattan Beach we'll be glad to have you." "I'd love to come to New York," I said. The beach was in California.

While the mayors were knocking back the vodka and preparing to fuck the hookers and have their pictures secretly taken by the KGB, I returned to our room with a bottle of "nature identical" soda water.

For three days we wandered after our guide through grey air and snowflakes in the direction of gold domes, churches of spilt blood, palaces and the landmark homes of great and approved Russian writers. On the day that we were to depart for Moscow the morning hours were designated as "free time." You could not buy a map of Leningrad, nor a guide to its transport system, but Eleni persuaded Sveta, our cheerful Intourist guide, to help her make a pilgrimage to Dostoyevsky's tomb in the Tivkin cemetery. We went alone. The grave, when we arrived, turned out to be a not too impressive bust of the writer fronting a plinth headed by a large cross. Dostoyevsky was fenced off by wrought iron, there were no flowers, this was not Jim Morrison at Pere Lachaise, and the bare branches of the surrounding trees advanced our sense of gloomy isolation. Then a boy appeared in a long coat and floppy eared fur hat. He addressed us in English. He said his name was Dmitry and that he liked Pink Floyd. He asked if when we got back to England we would send him some LP's. We said we would. He gave us his address and then he left.

We were late getting back to the hotel and Sveta was angry with us. As punishment she withheld the sandwiches that had been distributed to our fellow travellers to sustain them during the seven-hour train ride to Moscow. Once we were in our carriage (we hadn't been *that* late) a kind-hearted American couple tried to slip us some of their bread and cheese but Sveta spotted the transaction in progress and intervened. This was our gulag experience.

Angela, in a fur coat, her long white hair untrammelled, was on the platform to meet us. Sveta did not want to give her prisoners up, but fortunately her jurisdiction ended in Moscow and before the new guide could come to replace her we were down in the Metro, that marvelous chandeliered Soviet tribute to the worker's state, the Winter Palace for commuters. "We'll go to your hotel later," Angela said, "We have an invitation for dinner."

We travelled on the Zamoskvoretskaya line to Dinamo station whose white and gray marble tiled walls were interspersed with sport-themed bas-reliefs: a javelin thrower, a hurdler, a boxer. I was thrilled to be there. I knew that when we emerged onto Leningradsky Avenue we would see the great football stadium, home to Moscow Dynamo, where the world's greatest goalkeeper Lev Yashin had once stood between the sticks to parry and punch with his massive hands. From my experience with Magic Moments I knew well the magnificent solitude of that position. Neither Eleni nor Angela had any interest in football, their concentration was elsewhere, on Nabokov's haughtiness, or Bunin's dark avenues, or the poet whose lover in waiting wanted her to describe how she kissed and how men kissed her.

Our host for the evening was Zhenia Levitin who was, Angela told us, an old friend of hers who worked for the Pushkin Museum of Fine Art; a specialist on Rembrandt, he had published a number of articles in journals and introductions to books. Zhenia's apartment was several floors up via a rickety old Muscovite elevator. He greeted us at the door, a small man with a solemn look and large, slightly bulging, intense eyes behind black-framed glasses. In his tiny kitchen he served us chicken and bread then opened a bottle of wine. He went about his business of hospitality in a manner than was almost stern. I did not participate, of course, in the Russian conversation, but afterwards I learned that Zhenia had described how he had recently been refused an exit visa to visit Yugoslavia on the grounds that (a) he was a Jew, (b) he was not married, (c) he was not a member of the Communist party; whether these were the reasons officially given (to the extent that anything in those days was distinctly 'official' in the Soviet Union), or he just guessed that they were the operative reasons, Angela did not know. It was, I learned, a miserable fact of life for Zhenia that he could not go abroad. I don't know what Angela had told him about me but at one point when the conversation ebbed he stared hard at me and then asked, in English, if I had ever visited Israel. "Yes," I replied, "I have."

These were the years when the Jewish refusenik movement was at its peak and the Soviet authorities practiced a cruel bait and switch. Some Jews, a trickle, were allowed to leave, but more often application for a visa resulted in persecution, a lost job, or a beating: active dissent frequently brought imprisonment. I knew that Jews from the West visiting Russia often held clandestine meetings with courageous protestors and passed on smuggled prayer books and other banned material. I was not of their number, and felt a pang of guilt, a coward's remorse that my suitcase was clean for inspection. If Zhenia wanted to pursue our conversation he quickly thought better of it, nervous perhaps about the infamous listening devices in Soviet apartments. He never smiled throughout the evening, but he sang. At the end of our meal he began, slowly and firmly, a song that seemed to have many verses and which he sang to the end very solemnly.

In Moscow we saw Lenin in his mausoleum and visited the department store GUM, where one of the American women on our tour described the bra counter with its unadorned, uniform display of white cups as "like the Himalayas." On our last evening, when the cold felt like fifteen-pound lead weights on our heads and we regretted not having splurged on fur hats at one of the tourist Berioszka shops, Angela brought Eleni and me to dinner with Yevgeny Borisovich Pasternak, son of the great novelist Boris Pasternak. I have to admit that at this point in my life I had not read *Dr. Zhivago*, and knew it only as a movie in which, horribly, Omar Sharif had found and then lost the love of his life, Julie Christie, and everything had ended in tears and a hydroelectric station. Angela was in the midst of translating Boris Pasternak's *Safe Conduct* into English and there were, it seemed, numerous obstacles in the path of publication. Yevgeny Pasternak, strikingly handsome, bore an uncanny resemblance to pictures that I had seen of his father. He was an engineer by trade, a branch line away from the occupations of his father and grandfather Leonid, whose portraits covered the walls of the apartment. Several guests arrived; a samovar appeared on the table. The atmosphere was convivial, smoking, laughter, but the conversation was exclusively in Russian and I was a silent observer. Eventually one of the guests turned to me and asked in English who I preferred, Tolstoy or Dostoyevsky, and when I replied "Dostoyevsky" he said "Are you Jewish?" as if my answer had somehow predetermined that possibility. He went on to inform me that many Russian Orthodox priests in the city were in fact converted Jews, severely restricted in the practice of their first religion and searching for a spiritual outlet. "The priests are rabbis," he said. Later in the evening this same guest whispered to me, "This country is shit."

* * *

Seventeen years later I was in Israel on a visit. My first book of short stories, *Schoom*, had recently come out in the U.K. and as most of the tales were set in Jerusalem I had been invited to give a reading in the city. My friend Gabriel Levin, a poet and translator, asked me if I wanted to go with him to meet a recent Russian immigrant whom he had been introduced to by a local artist, a Russian painter. The man had arrived in Israel a few months earlier, Gaby told me, and was living with his wife, a former student, in a depressing apartment in Gilo on the outskirts of the city near Bethlehem. The man had been crippled by a stroke back in Moscow, and was confined to a wheelchair. He couldn't walk and had use of only one hand. He had been told that physical therapy could improve his condition but he was resisting the treatment.

We took the bus to Gilo. I entered the room, and there was Zhenia. His wife, whose name, it turned out, was also Zhenia (Evgenia), stood next to the wheelchair. She was considerably younger than her husband, tall with pale blue eyes, high, Slavic cheeks with a touch of pink, and straight straw-blonde hair. Later I learned that she had been first his student, then his lover, in Moscow. Zhenia stared at me with his bulging eyes. "Zhenia!" I said, "I can't believe it's you. We met in Moscow many years ago. You asked me about Israel." He looked at me for a long time; everyone in the room was silent, and then, with what seemed like an extraordinary effort to speak, he said, "You came with beautiful Greek girl."

The afternoon progressed; blonde Zhenia, visibly devoted to her husband, catered to his every need and then, when he grew tired, lifted him from the wheelchair in her strong arms and carried him to a day bed set up by a window in the small room. The living conditions seemed not much different to what he had known in Russia. Apparently their earnings came from the piecemeal selling of the few drawings from Zhenia's private collection that he had managed to bring out of Russia.

Zhenia was still at once strangely stern and delicate, fragile and serious as I had known him in Moscow in 1975. Blonde Zhenia told us that Nadezhda Mandelstam—whom they'd visited from time to time when in Moscow—used to call him "the little sparrow." Because of the odd affinity I felt with Zhenia, as if I had known him far, far better than I did, I took it upon myself to try to persuade him to pursue a course of physical therapy. "Gaby tells me that if you did, you could really improve your health," I said. Again, he stared at me before responding, "If you continue to talk to me like that I will begin not to like you." The sun, having reached its zenith, collapsed into the room through shades as a tired warrior: dusty, impeached, as if it, and not Zhenia, hadn't done enough. Two years later he died following a massive second stroke.

Only recently, when I began to write this book, I contacted Angela to ask for her memories of Zhenia. She sent me a long, wonderful letter which included a description of taking the two Zhenias to the Spring Fair at Midsummer Common in Cambridge on his only visit to England in 1989. There she persuaded Zhenia to ride on the merry-go-round: "I looked round from my horseback to see that he was safe, and there he was, bouncing up and down on one of the painted gallopers, looking as serious and focused as if in the midst of giving a lecture."

*   *   *

Three factors began to endear me to Oxford when I returned. First, after I took the Bibliography/English Hands exams, I was free to pursue my studies unencumbered by additional requirements; second, I met a lot of interesting Americans; and third, I began to play soccer for St. Catherine's.

Americans at Oxford in the late 1960s and 1970s, including some of Bill Clinton's old pals, have occasionally complained about their virtual segregation from the British students, a division made wider during Vietnam and the immediate post-Vietnam years by the same dull-witted identification of individual Americans with the activities of their government that so isolated Lowell at Essex. (It was the same decades later all over Europe for American students during the Bush Junior years.) But for the Jewish students, Americans were infinitely appealing. I became friends with Leon Wieseltier, who was not only American but seriously Jewish as well. But there were others, some Jewish, some not, from Michigan, Wisconsin, and Connecticut, who were able, simply by virtue of their extreme otherness, to accord me the illusion that I was an authentic Oxonian, not there under false pretenses at all.

My supervisor, Larzer Ziff, was also American, and also new to the place. In the 1970s, the university had decided to acknowledge that the American literature of the previous two centuries constituted more (although not a lot more) than an irrelevant blip on the great screen of English writing. Faculty with specialization in the area were appointed, and students were permitted, if not exactly encouraged, to pursue some study of the alien texts. Even so, the most frequent response I got when describing my studies at Oxford was the terribly witty "American literature? *Is* there any American literature?"

At the time, as far as I was concerned, there was *only* American literature (and this had been true for some time). The reason had less to do with Hawthorne, Melville, and Emily Dickinson than with Saul Bellow, Bernard Malamud, and Philip Roth. With them the sense of intimacy was profound. At Oxford, the most influential Jews I came across were the characters Charlie Citrine, Sy Levin, and Nathan Zuckerman. Similarly, I enjoyed sitting in the Bodleian Library reading Jewish-American novels from the 1930s by Mike Gold, Meyer Levin, or Daniel Fuchs. Their names, and the titles of their books—*Jews Without Money, Yehuda, Summer in*

Williamsburg—also seemed like an affront to the old stones.

For two years, I lived in the village of Iffley, some two miles from the city of Oxford and from my college. Most mornings I biked over a pretty, well-kept lock, its quayside decorated with tubs of flowers, and down the towpath that ran beside the River Isis all the way into town. There was very little that I *had* to do: there were no classes or seminars at the graduate level and, post-Bibliography and English Hands, attendance at lectures was optional. Like almost everyone else, I exercised my option— except once for a guest lecture by George Steiner. In English universities in those years, the hand that guided the student had a light touch, so light that were it not for the faint checks in the margin of an essay or the single, almost indecipherable scrawled comment at the end, the student might well think that he or she was essentially self-taught.

If there was a party going on at Oxford, it wasn't likely to be political (except at one particular college, Balliol) or wired to the larger world's zeitgeist in any other way; it would be some time-less champagne-and-strawberry drift downstream and, appealing as that sounds, the likelihood was that one wouldn't be invited anyway. In three years at Oxford, I didn't meet a single Bright Young Thing: no drugged-out baroness or suicidal earl, no scion of a family who owned a fair-sized chunk of England. This was partly because my college was a designated middle-class zone (the buildings were modern), and partly because I was a post-graduate, and the essential Oxford experience remained at the earlier, undergraduate level where merit was not the only criteria for entrance (Prince Charles was shoehorned into Cambridge), and where what used to be called a "gentleman's third" (something like graduating with a 2.5 GPA) was held in higher regard than the vulgar careerism and nerdy obsessions that pushed people toward further degrees. In any case, the denizens of Christ Church and the other colleges that catered primarily to the aristocracy were phantasmal to me. I only knew they were there because I read about them in gossip magazines.

I hung out with Leon Wieseltier and his girlfriend Hilary, who became friends with Eleni and also with other "foreigners": Richard Haass, who went on to become president of the United States Council on Foreign Relations; Katya Krausova, a Czech in exile who became a filmmaker; and the Israeli poet and translator T. Carmi, who was at Oxford to complete his ten years of work on *The Penguin Book of Hebrew Verse*. Carmi had been born Carmi Charny, but everyone called him only by the last name of this adopted pseudonym. His friendship was to be life-altering for me.

When we met, among all the veils of illusion on offer to ambitious youth, I had plucked the mask of promising young poet. I wore it with pride, although my output and talent were incommensurate with self-assurance. I had shown Carmi some poems and he had been extraordinarily gracious with work that, when I look at it now, is beyond embarrassing. Toward the end of his Herculean labors on the *Penguin Book*, Carmi claimed to have grown nervous about some of the English locutions that he had used in the introduction, for although he was American-born and had lived on and off in the United States for many years, Hebrew had been the first language in his New York Zionist household. He enlisted my help for some minor editing that in truth he didn't really need: he was simply being kind.

* * *

Soccer at Oxford was pleasurable and pampered. I played, at different times, for both St. Catherine's first and second teams.

Everything surrounding the games was high-end and cozy—manicured fields, cider in dimpled glasses provided post-match by university employees back in the clubhouse. Partly because St. Catz's traditionally drew a large chunk of its student body from the Midlands and the North of England, our teams were really good. The soccer fields of Oxford were one place where I felt completely at home in the university environment, and I think it was the only way I made my mark on the college.

Somehow, perhaps because I had arrived in the middle of the year, I slipped through a lot of bureaucratic and administrative cracks. I was the only student never invited to "high table"—dinner with bigwigs from the college—and decades later when I began to receive requests for donations from a St. Catherine's newly alive to alumni giving, I discovered that I was listed as "Miss J. M. Wilson" on the college register. "Miss J. M. Wilson," it seemed, owed the library a considerable amount in late fees, but it turned out not to be my female doppelgänger, but a student from around my time named Janet Wilson. Eventually the college sorted it all out—I hadn't imagined being at Oxford after all, but my sense of ghostliness at the place has never entirely dissolved. On the soccer field, however, I felt, as always, entirely present.

* * *

In 1976, around the time that the Oxford Union, with Benazir Bhutto (then a student at St. Catz) as its treasurer, debated whether or not Israel was "politically necessary and morally justified" (the vote narrowly favored the continued existence of the Jewish state), I learned that I had received a grant to spend a semester at Columbia University in New York City.

Of the six Jewish boys I knew from Kilburn Grammar who

had gone to Oxford or Cambridge before me, three had left the country soon after graduating, two to go to the United States and one to Israel. It has always seemed to me that Kilburn molded a kind of excessive personality, one that wasn't really suited to England, or to what England had in mind in those years for brash, unbuttoned, street-wise but militantly intellectual Jewish boys. Oxford and Cambridge seemed designed to calm everybody down, to "put you in your place," both literally and figuratively. At Kilburn Grammar, we had invented ourselves in the hot crucible of the sixties as strange, hybrid creatures, big-brained but running on fuel provided by Keith Moon's pounding drums. With its schizophrenic, ersatz public-school environment, the school could not contain our energy, but Oxford, the real thing, could. Sometimes I felt that Oxford's buildings themselves, the thick college walls, the enclosed quads, towers, and Gothic arches, seemed to possess an absorbent capacity, an ability to assimilate rebellious natures. The shaping influence of the place was strong, and to counteract it I evolved in my mind a powerful symbolic alternative, one that seemed to reflect the consciousness that Kilburn Grammar and, to a certain extent, the University of Essex had patterned: the farraginous city of New York.

Aubade: I'm playing for St. Catherine's against Balliol. The air is heavy with the scents of autumn, and the sky's tinged red where the sun is sinking behind the plane trees, sycamores and oaks with their burning leaves. The season is on fire. We beat Balliol. We kick their ass, although "kick their ass" is not yet in my vocabulary. There's even a crowd on the sidelines; the first eleven come to cheer on their understudies. I score twice in a 3–0 victory. It feels great. I don't know it, but it's my last game in England. I'm off to the U.S. of A., land of No-Interest-In-Soccer, the only one like it on the planet.

Chapter 10

I arrived in New York on July 2, 1976, two nights before the bicentennial celebration. Firecrackers had already begun to fizz from the stoops and sidewalks and fireworks illuminated the sky over the city; tall ships were on their way down the Hudson. It was a perfect immigrants' welcome. A friend of Leon Wieseltier's from Columbia, Tom Sawicki, had kindly agreed to loan me his room in a shared apartment on the Upper West Side for a few weeks while he was away for the summer.

On my first morning, I went into Tom's Restaurant on Broadway (later made famous by *Seinfeld*). I stared at the menu for a long time, overwhelmed by the range of cheap breakfasts on offer. Eventually, a matronly waitress approached my table, leaned over me, and said, "Talk to me, baby, I'll listen to you."

Everybody treated me very kindly because I was from England, and thought I was smart because I went to Oxford. Nobody I met seemed to have any idea that Jews lived in countries other than the United States and Israel. After a lifetime of being identified first and foremost by my religion, I found myself stripped of that primary identity. I was now a "limey," a "bloke," an "old chap," and all those other boring nicknames and catchphrases (most of them obsolete) that my new American acquaintances had picked up from Masterpiece Theatre.

On the outside, I was a graduate student from Oxford over to spend a semester at Columbia. My thesis, seriously unfocused at this time (and for all time), purported to be something about radical Jewish-American writing in the 1930s. There were books in Butler Library that I needed to read. On the inside, something was bubbling that had first stirred when, at the age of fourteen, in the summer of 1964, my friend Robert Lipman had passed his copy of *Franny and Zooey* on to me. We were spending a fortnight at my Uncle Simey's strictly kosher Happy Holiday School (because of its awful associations, the word "camp" was not used to describe the summer vacations of Jewish children in England). It rained almost every day and I devoured the novel in two sittings.

It was through Salinger that I began deeply to imagine Jewish life in America. I had previously read *The Catcher in the Rye* and been both delighted and baffled by it. The bafflement came because I couldn't imagine what Holden's little brother Allie's baseball mitt looked like. I had never seen one, and Salinger didn't bother with a lengthy description. However, neither the Glass family in *Franny and Zooey* nor Moses Herzog, whom I came across a year later in Saul Bellow's great novel *Herzog*, prepared me for the Portnoys of Philip Roth's *Portnoy's Complaint*. Almost throughout 1969, it seemed, I had engaged in a yearlong shouting match with my mother about *that* book. The arguments were fueled, it must be admitted, by my relationship with Pat and, after we broke up, by my continued intimate friendships with gentile girls including Pat's best friend Sheila McNally (Lorna had arrived and departed while my mother was on a long vacation in South Africa visiting her brother Harold).

Portnoy's Complaint became the sacred text of my life. It mattered more to me than any of the "banned books" by D. H. Lawrence, Henry Miller, and the Marquis de Sade that, for reasons determined by the vast prairies of open time that I spent alone in my room with my brother Stephen's "library," I had gulped down by the age of fourteen and returned to frequently as the occasion demanded.

Portnoy's Complaint, if only she could see it, was the book of my mother's life. Sophie Portnoy WAS Doris Wilson;: the only difference as far as I could tell was that Doris Wilson had an English accent. Like Sophie Portnoy, Doris Wilson stopped at nothing to protect her youngest and most vulnerable child from the temptations and dangers presented by the gentile world. If private letters needed to be opened and read, so be it; if phone calls had to be listened in on, then what is wrong with that? "I *hate* that book," my mother screamed, and she actually had tears in her eyes. "I *hate* that Philip Roth. Horrible horrible horrible book." To which I could only muster the lame and hopeless reply, "But you haven't read it." The tension and discomfort persisted so long as I remained in England.

I think now that I came to America not so much to further my academic career but, encouraged by my reading of Philip Roth, to become a Jewish writer. I did not believe that I could become one in England, certainly not in any meaningful way, but these larger ambitions were probably hidden even from myself. I was still writing poetry, but the only fictions I created were directed toward impressing girls in one of the two bars on Broadway that had been recommended to me: The Gold Rail and The West End.

*   *   *

One day as I was crossing the Columbia campus in the pouring rain, I met a fellow student, Allison Funk, who really was a poet. She introduced me to the delights of the Ninety-Second Street YMHA. We went almost every Monday night to see and hear the great poets read, Elizabeth Bishop and a now repatriated Robert Lowell among them. Allison had recently converted to Judaism. I can't remember why, but a Jewish boyfriend was in the picture somewhere. Jews and New York: the terms were more or less synonymous in my mind (as in everyone else's), and it was a wonderful feeling after a lifetime of minority self-effacement to be a part of the loud majority.

On an unseasonably wintry Saturday night in early October, close to midnight, I helped my friend Barak Berkowitz move a large double bed from 110th Street to his new apartment on 106th. We rolled the bed on its clattery casters down Broadway. I had taken a shower only a few minutes before going out, and the freezing night air turned my hair to ice. Nobody, cops included, seemed to care that we were blocking the road. There were self-dramatizing groups and individuals up and down the sidewalk: idlers and chatterers of all ages, students, boozers, panhandlers, partygoers, all of them mixed, merged, colorful, juicy, and bathed in light like the starstruck fruit and flowers in the bodegas. I felt the way F. Scott Fitzgerald describes in *The Crack Up* when he recalls the heady Manhattan days of his first great literary success: "And lastly from that period I remember riding in a taxi one afternoon between very tall buildings under a mauve and rosy sky; I began to bawl because I had everything I wanted and knew I would never be so happy again." Only instead of thinking that I would never be so happy again, it occurred to me that, whether as principals or bit players in the city's general theater, I had never in my life seen Jewish people have so much fun.

Three months earlier, I had spent an extraordinary two weeks with Barak on his father's marijuana estate in Willits, California. We were there, ostensibly, to help Mr. Berkowitz build his dream house. In the early seventies after meeting Timothy Leary, Mr. Berkowitz had quit his job on Wall Street and taken off for Mendocino County and the cash-crop farmer's life. He and Barak's mother were long separated, and his father was presently living with a long-limbed blonde woman named See-Joy in a teepee they had erected on his land. See-Joy, who was only a few years older than we were, liked to walk around naked, and we all bathed together in the creek that ran in a dip below our encampment. There was a fence, and some barking dogs to keep unwanted visitors away. We didn't get much building done. The days started late for Mr. Berkowitz, and we were all (except for Barak, who never touched the stuff) stoned quite a bit of the time.

New York is, of course, a city of wonderful distractions, heightened to an almost impossible degree when you are in your twenties, and, following the old Nottingham path through the forest, I made the best of it by not attending any classes at all— they were, in any case, optional for me. Primarily, I was at Columbia to conduct research in Butler Library with its famously sexy stacks, where switching the light on or off down an aisle of books was up to you. No one at Oxford knew or cared what I was up to. There was still a governing aristocratic belief at the English university that simple immersion in the culture of a foreign country was probably education enough. When the British government realized that middle-class students were benefiting in this way from their Department of Education grants, it more or less shut the program down.

*   *   *

109

On my way out of Butler Library, I would sometimes see students playing soccer on the quad's green. To my astonishment the players included girls. How could this be? The girls seemed neither worse nor better than the boys: they were all uniformly terrible, shooting, passing, and tackling in a performance of impressive awkwardness. H. G. Bassinger's book *Friday Night Lights* reports in its coda the experience of a great high school footballer who, after acceptance to Harvard, joins the college football team only to quit soon after because the game doesn't resemble the one he has known in Odessa, Texas. The Ivy League just isn't tough enough. Columbia quad soccer didn't look like soccer to me, much as I'm sure the basketball I sometimes played in the gym at Kilburn Grammar would not have appeared to be basketball to any American observer.

To supplement my grant, I worked as a waiter in the Hungarian Pastry Shop on Amsterdam Avenue. I was the first (and last) male waiter they ever employed. I know this because I revisited the café last year and the owner, after some prodding, remembered me, and how I had soured him on male employees. After work I headed mostly for The Gold Rail where Bruce Springsteen's *Spirit in the Night* seemed to play in an endless loop on the jukebox. There, watching TV at the bar or from a booth, I tried to figure out baseball. Baseball wasn't methadone for my addiction to soccer, but it helped a little to relieve the yearning and the pain that derived from living in a city that, in 1976, didn't seem to know what English (or any other) soccer was, let alone show games on television.

It was in The Gold Rail that I saw the Yankees play Kansas City in the deciding fifth game of the 1976 ALCS playoffs. In the bottom of the ninth of a tie game, Chris Chambliss hit a massive home run. The crowd, both at the game and in the bar, went crazy. There was a stiff wind blowing at Yankee Stadium, and pieces of paper, like tumbleweed, blew across the pitcher's mound. In one moment, although I knew almost nothing about baseball, I felt that I understood everything.

In February 1977 I published my first piece of writing in the United States, a review for *Commentary* magazine of *The Paris Review Interviews, Third Series*. I was hard at work on a review of Lionel Trilling's reissued novel *The Middle of the Journey* for the magazine *Midstream* when I received a phone call from my friend Carmi. He had learned that a position was about to open up to teach twentieth-century American literature in the English Department at the Hebrew University of Jerusalem. Was I interested? I didn't want to leave New York, but my semester in America was, in any case, drawing to an end.

On my last Saturday in New York, I took a bicycle ride with Barak up to The Cloisters. It was February 26, 1977, my twenty-sixth birthday. Late winter in New York that year felt like early spring; the air was warm enough, the sky a blue coin of its own minting, and the wind over the Hudson blew sweetly toward the Palisades. In the Heather Garden of Fort Tryon Park the dog-tooth violets, peonies, and poppies that I would come to see years later were hidden under frozen soil. I wandered through the halls past the Unicorn Tapestries. My friends from Columbia were kindly throwing a farewell party for me that night at the "the Aubergine house," their graduate accommodation on West 113 Street near the Symposium restaurant.

The following morning, I learned that Tottenham had just lost 2–0 at home to Newcastle. For once in my life, I really didn't care.

Chapter 11

In April, a few days before Passover, I traveled to Jerusalem to interview for the teaching post at Hebrew University. Carmi had arranged a meeting with Baruch Hochman, the chairman of the English Department. The position, if I got it, would begin in the fall.

I stayed with Carmi and his sculptor wife, Tamara. I was in awe of Carmi's setup, which seemed to have sprung unaltered from my own generally distorting but vivid romantic imagination. His old stone house was halfway up a sloping street in Abu Tor, a sleepy neighborhood off the main road to Bethlehem that still featured open space between the homes: small areas of high grass and rocks bordered by eucalyptus trees and scattered with wildflowers. Outside the basement apartment at 10 Rehov Aminadav, an old woman fed scrawny chickens in a broad courtyard. At the side were stairs that led to a roseate iron door adorned with a raised pattern of nippled dots in small circles; a Boccherini cello concerto issued through the open windows, while sunlight flowed in the opposite direction. Carmi's German shepherd, Dag, roused from his mid-afternoon stupor, barked like crazy in the garden. "It's a snake," Carmi said calmly, pushing open the door to the garden and looking over it. "He's found a snake." Perfect!

Carmi stood framed by the doorway in an oblong of light that seemed to represent the transcendent space to which his poems aspired. He was fifty-one. He had a solid reputation, although perhaps more as a scholar and translator than as a poet. His poems, laconic, guarded, literary, cleverly allusive, were not universally admired, certainly not in the way of his internationally loved contemporary Yehuda Amichai. From my point of view, everything about him was ideal. He smoked and coughed dramatically. His voice had a tenebrous roughness calibrated by two packs of TIME (the cheap Israeli cigarette) a day. Even his hair, raked high and back like the head of a stiff paintbrush soaked in gray, seemed to bespeak the life of art, if only because it revealed a daunting Shakespearean forehead.

To complete the picture, there was Carmi's history of personal heroism, rarely alluded to by the poet but readily available if you wanted as I did to take a bus ride to the British Council Library in the Terra Sancta building and peruse accounts of the battle for Jerusalem during the Israeli War of Independence in 1948. Carmi, twenty-three years old then and recently arrived in Palestine after working two and a half years in Paris at a home for the displaced children of Holocaust victims, had joined the Haganah. Within months, he was lugging a Beza machine gun to a rock outcropping near Sheikh Jarrah, ready to give his life in a do-or-die attempt to hold back the Arab Legion. He had taken out one armored car and damaged two others. The tiny force to which he belonged had lost more than half its men but, through a combination of luck, guile, and astonishing bravery under fire, had emerged victorious. Behind the rock next to Carmi, his closest friend lay with his head sundered as if parted by a meat axe.

I sat reading these accounts in the incongruous English atmosphere of the library—a woman in a straw hat was returning two novels by Iris Murdoch—and I thought of Yeats's lines in memory of his doomed friend, the Renaissance man, Major Robert Gregory: "Soldier, scholar, horseman, he, / ... / What made us dream that he could comb grey hair?" But Carmi *had* lived to comb gray hair, and he had maintained his military bearing. He walked with his shoulders back and his chest puffed out, as if by standing straight he could put behind him the entire bent and crooked history of the Jewish diaspora. How could I not be impressed? Both New York and Jerusalem offered attractive ways of being Jewish in the world that I had barely been able to imagine in England.

*   *   *

I met with Professor Hochman and all went well. Much of Israeli society at that time functioned around what is known as "protecsia," influence through connections of a certain kind, usually among well-educated Ashkenazi Jews, a practice endemic in a culture with a small population. (This was in the days before the emergence of a handful of powerful multimillionaire families, the Israeli equivalent of contemporary Russian oligarchs, whom Tel Aviv's tent city occupants would target for particular vilification in the summer of 2011.) It wasn't clear to me that I ever had any competitors for the job for which I had applied. Actually, I hadn't "applied" for anything. I was simply introduced to Professor Hochman, had a long conversation with him, and showed him some of my writing: the bulk of my application materials were presented only *after* I had already been informally offered the job.

A week went by at Carmi's. At night there were small social

gatherings around a coffee table in the front room. The local visitors, who would arrive around nine, materialized in the house without knocking, and frequently, I understood, without having been invited. Everyone enjoyed this studied informality, the appearance of spontaneity and looseness. Thrillingly the guests were invariably from the worlds of art and literature, although this fact hardly erased the awkwardness I felt when the conversation inevitably drifted into Hebrew, and I was left grinning and nodding my head to the unknown music of the language. In the space of a week, I met the great painter Avigdor Arikha, who was a close friend of Samuel Beckett, and the poet Dan Pagis, a Holocaust survivor, like Arikha, whose five-line poem "Written in Pencil in the Sealed Railway Car" remains the most succinct and powerful expression of the horror that I have ever read. There was also a slew of visiting foreigners. One Friday night, an English couple, the husband a painter, the wife a poet, came for dinner. Like me they had been in the city for a fortnight. Both their names were familiar to me: they were British culture figures from the second or maybe third tier—not the American heavy hitters like Edmund Wilson, Robert Lowell, and Bob Dylan whose visits to Jerusalem Carmi had amusingly described to an entranced crowd in the snug of The King's Head pub in Oxford. For this was 1977, and the big-shot foreign writers who, in the aftermath of plucky Israel's victory in the Six Day War, had made the city a must-see stop like Paris or Florence on the travel itinerary now, after war-machine Israel's Yom Kippur triumph, abruptly scattered to be replaced by lower profiles. Israel, as Lowell himself told Carmi in a letter, was back "on the wrong side of the stockade."

Tami, wearing a long, white, embroidered Bedouin dress, refilled the olive dish. Carmi topped up the whiskey glasses. The delights and truancies of language were his favorite topics of discussion. There was much talk of etymology and definition interrupted by frequent forays into the study to check dictionaries for the root or meaning of certain words. My compatriots loved it. And so did I, theoretically anyway, until I realized toward midnight on this ritually insecure Sabbath evening (there were no candles, no braided challah) that, to my shame, I was profoundly, unutterably, and completely bored.

The next day I went in search of people my own age. Across the street I found Gabriel Levin, who lived with his wife Maria in a small stone house surrounded by scented pines. Gaby, American-born but educated in France and Israel, was also a poet, although, like myself, at the beginning stages. In fact the whole street seemed devoted to poetry. At the top of Aminadav, in a kind of wasteland that was officially a compound owned by the Russian Orthodox Church, lived the Anglo-Israeli poet Dennis Silk. Dennis's hut, for it was no more than that, housed his collection of puppets, dolls, and objects for which he wrote and produced plays. His poems, sui generis, curious, economical, eccentric, and possessed, like Dennis himself, of an ascetic discipline, were also political. He wanted to save the land of Israel/Palestine from marauding extremists on both sides. For some reason that I could never discover, Dennis and Carmi, near neighbors, were not on speaking terms. I think, like my mother and her sister Rene, they had long ago forgotten whatever it was that they had argued about, but the bad feeling remained.

The job was offered and I took it. All that remained was to secure a work visa, return to England to collect my stuff, and see whether or not Eleni would agree to move with me to Israel.

* * *

London's Jewish Agency for Israel didn't approve of my relationship with Eleni any more than my mother, and its bureaucrats more or less refused to support her application for a visa. We approached instead the open-minded sophisticates at the Israeli embassy. They were happy to help and issued me a "Visiting Foreign Expert" visa. This was much better, I thought, than inhabiting the role of a regular-old-returning Jew with all the other riff-raff. It also meant that I was not on track to become a citizen. As a "Visiting Expert," I could not get tax breaks but neither was I en route to army duty. It never became clear what I was an expert in: the history of Tottenham Hotspur FC was probably the closest I could claim to a specialized field of knowledge.

Eleni and I had been together for seven years but we only lasted four months in Jerusalem. On a trip to the oasis of Nuweiba in the Sinai desert Eleni left our tent in the middle of the night, ran to the water's edge, and disappeared into the sea. I went after her, calling her name, but I couldn't see her. I don't know what her intentions were but she soon reappeared further up the beach looking quite cheerful, but when I approached she said, "You didn't try to save me."

On Christmas Eve 1977, we went to Bethlehem and sat in Manger Square. The atmosphere was charged. There were Israeli soldiers on the rooftops; earlier in the evening, someone had chucked a grenade. The night was cold but we had 777 brandy to fortify us; a Felliniesque parade of religious dignitaries filed into the Church of the Nativity, one of them holding a plastic baby Jesus in his arms. A Scottish choir, kilts swaying, knees knocking in the frigid wind, sang "Once in Royal David's City." All around the square vendors were hard at work selling olive wood camels and crosses, mother-of-pearl brooches, and hot kebabs. Two men from the West German embassy who didn't want to abandon their beers slipped us their entry tickets to Midnight Mass. I passed on mine. Eleni went in with our friend John, a native Minnesotan out in Jerusalem to work as a master printer in the Burston Graphic Center. They never reappeared.

I walked and stumbled back to Jerusalem through darkened olive groves. I felt, I have to admit, more relief than loss. Eleni and I had been together since we were twenty; we both knew that something had gone wrong in our relationship but neither of us was very good at getting free. It took an apocalyptic night in Bethlehem to do the trick.

* * *

I lived at 3 Bezalel Street in a wonderful apartment secured for me by Carmi's protecsia. It was on the second floor of a house on the grounds of the Bezalel Academy of Arts and Design. I thought it the most beautiful dwelling in the world. At the turn of the twentieth century the old stone house with a walled in garden had been home to Boris Schatz, founder of Jerusalem's secular, subversive Bezalel Art School. Boris's son Lilik, a sculptor and metalworker (he designed the gates of the President's house), was my landlord. He lived on the ground floor with his wife Louise, a painter whose sister Eve McClure had once been married to Henry Miller. For a while in the late 1940's Lilik, Henry and the McClure sisters had lived the Boho life together in Big Sur. Lilik and Louise had helped Henry to build a swimming pool. Lilik once told me how he had inset tiles, shells, and coins all around the sides. "So beautiful," Henry had said, "You can bury me in this." Henry had devoted a chapter to Lilik in his book *My Bike and other Friends*. When I met the Schatzs, they had been living together in Jerusalem for more than twenty years and it was thrilling to discover that Louise's Hebrew was even worse than mine.

My apartment belonged to Lilik's younger sister Zahara, a painter who was on an extended sojourn in California. On the floor below me there was one other tenant, Max, a retired sailor from the U.S. merchant marine. Every morning Max, who walked with a seaman's gait, watered the garden, as efficiently as he had once swabbed the decks, and released the scent of oleander and roses to my balcony. Some nights in summer I dragged my mattress out and slept under the bright stars and the overhanging branches of a gnarled olive tree: cyclamen grew in the crevices of the balcony's exterior walls and thick-stemmed pink geraniums twisted their heads in my window boxes. On Fridays, before Shabbat, the carpet-beaters, wives and daughters, came out onto their balconies to spank the dust from household rugs in a last great crescendo of activity before the quiet of evening.

Max had a telephone and I didn't. After Eleni returned to England, our most painful conversations were conducted while Max washed dishes in his sink. In the evenings he and I often played Scrabble together. He told me about his life on container ships and how once, when his ship had developed some serious mechanical problems, the other sailors had wanted to dump him at a port: the only Jew on board, he was considered to be a bad-luck Jonah.

* * *

Recently, while on a trip to Israel, I decided to revisit 3 Bezalel Street.

Almost thirty-five years after I had moved in, I stood before the wooden door in the wall that led to the secret garden. There, set in stone, was a plaque that listed the names, dates and occupations of the Schatz family members who had once lived in the house. Lilik's bracket was particularly poignant as he had died during my tenancy, and in the last months of his life Max and I had gone to a clinic to stockpile blood for him in preparation for a surgery that, sadly, never took place.

As far as I know, no one outside the Schatz family ever lived in the house on 3 Bezalel Street except for Max, myself, and, briefly, Eleni. Of course, our names were not on the plaque, why would they be? The commemoration informed the passer-by of significant individuals who had made a vast contribution to the world of their home country's art. It was not an inventory of those who happened to have lived at that address.

When, in 1883, ten-year old Willa Cather first encountered the open range prairie of Nebraska, no trees, no telephone poles, no fencing, no nothing, she experienced what she later described as "a kind of erasure of personality." Geography can do that to you, but so can history. Reading the plaque I experienced a Catheresque erasure. Where was I? The question was not narcissistic (I hope) but rather evolved from an uncanny sense of absence. The house had once contained my physical presence, and I contained my memory of the house. If there had been no plaque I think I would have felt no inkling of erasure. On the other hand it was an enormous relief not to be on the plaque; after all, most frequently only the homes of the dead are marked this way.

But what about Max who had held me together when I was falling apart? His fellow sailors had wanted to dump him off their ship and here he was, dumped again. I wished I could have added his name to the brass plate: Max Freedman, big-hearted old man of the sea who worked the container ships on the Pacific route from San Francisco to Java also lived here from 1967 to 1982.

*　*　*

I lived on Bezalel Street for a year and pursued my job as a lowly instructor in the English Department at Hebrew University. I taught Introduction to Literary Genres, and I loved the job. Some of the students didn't speak English that well but they made up for that deficiency with high intelligence and enthusiasm. I learned a lot. There were mainly girls in the classes, and most of them had recently completed their army service.

Shortly before I started teaching at Hebrew University I had secured a second job in the English Department of the University of Tel Aviv. There I taught an English literature survey course of the Beowulf to Virginia Woolf variety. I commuted to the job with a colleague who lived near me in Jerusalem, Ephraim Edelstein. Ephraim had a car, but his license had been revoked, so he needed a driver. Ephraim was an irrepressible individual: a wildly expressive young gay man in a country where homosexuality was still largely hidden. He had an American boyfriend, Stevie, but that didn't stop him from cruising certain parks in Tel Aviv after his classes were done for the day. I would have to pick him up at pre-assigned spots toward which he would stagger at the appointed hour, emerging from the cover of trees and bushes drunk and happy. Ephraim taught Jane Austen and his scholarship was focused on her characters' conflicts between passion and duty. Jane's women always flirted with passion but in the end went for duty; Ephraim's life was the other way round. On the way back to Jerusalem we would stop in Ramle to eat mixed grill in pita bread. He propositioned me once every few weeks, and if we picked up a male hitchhiker he would come on to him too; he especially enjoyed the challenge if we picked up a Hasid. He was brilliant and funny and he did

121

a lot of drugs. He once said to me, "It's crazy to be alive."

Ephraim was murdered in New York City in 1983. The details are murky but I believe he had let someone into his apartment that he shouldn't have. The killer hit him over the head with a blunt object. Ephraim was in a coma for some weeks, and then he died.

I didn't want a car in Jerusalem so I bought a bicycle, which everyone, including the man who sold it to me, seemed to think was insane in that hilly city. I also acquired a shrink, a lovely Argentinian woman named Lea whose office was full of books on death and dying: she was professionally attached to an oncology center at Hadassah hospital. The texts on her shelves were therapy in themselves, a weekly reminder of the relative insignificance of my own problems.

* * *

One late summer afternoon after a session, I was sitting in a café on Emek Refaim (the Valley of the Ghosts) in the German Colony when a friend announced, "Rehavia has fallen." He meant that our secular, lefty, liberal, intellectual, art-filled, elite world had collapsed in yet another Jerusalem neighborhood and was now to be concentrated in a tiny area around the street where we were sitting. He meant that lots of Orthodox Jews had moved into the environs of Rehavia. Jerusalem was changing rapidly: Israelis known to be more fervent about God and religion were moving up and in. This demographic shift affected one particular aspect of my life that most middle-class Israelis couldn't have cared less about: soccer.

Unlike the United States, Israel was a soccer nation. It had a proper league and a more than adequate national team that had reached the World Cup Finals in Mexico in 1970, securing a creditable draw with Italy before elimination in the group stages. Soccer supporters in Israel, however, were almost exclusively drawn from the poorer Sephardic Jewish community, immigrants, mostly, from Arab countries. For everyone else, basketball was the dominant sport. Sephardic Jews loved soccer, but a large segment of the population was also observantly religious, albeit in, from the Western orthodox perspective, a sometimes quirky fashion. Despite rabbinical disapproval the government of Israel, in an attempt to accommodate both Saturday soccer (Sunday is a weekday in Israel) and religious sensitivities, permitted games to be played on the Sabbath, but only if tickets were purchased beforehand.

Since my arrival in Israel I had been going to games at the old stadium in the Katamon neighborhood, home to Hapoel Katamon Jerusalem FC. Founded in the 1930s, Hapoel was a sporting offshoot of leftist labor organizations. Its bitter crosstown rival was Beitar Jerusalem, whose supporters identified with right-wing nationalist groups (and still do: as recently as 2012 a group of Beitar fans protested the arrival of their team's first Moslem player, Zaur Sadayev, a Chechen, by destroying trophies in the clubhouse, chanting racist slogans, and leaving the stadium when Sadayev scored).

Ideological opposition between rival teams is not uncommon in the world of soccer; you might think, at a different point in history, of socialist Barcelona and fascist Real Madrid. More common, however, is religious division. In Britain, large cities with two teams have often, and sometimes still do, attract support along sectarian lines. In Glasgow, Catholics traditionally support Celtic while Protestants are for Rangers; in Liverpool, Catholics tend to support Liverpool and Protestants Everton; Manchester United's crowd was once predominantly Catholic and Manchester City's

Protestant. The "Catholic" teams always play in red or green and the "Protestant" teams in blue. In Jerusalem, Hapoel played in red and black and Beitar in yellow. It's possible that the red signified an early socialist link for Hapoel, but I couldn't figure out Beitar's yellow and nobody was able to enlighten me.

The home crowd in Katamon, like all soccer crowds, was raucous, abusive to the visiting team and, on occasion, potentially threatening to anybody at all who happened to be in the vicinity. But in general, and certainly compared to crowds in England or Italy, Jerusalem fans were an enthusiastic but sober group.

It was the British who first brought soccer to Palestine, and during the Mandate there were British, Jewish, and Arab clubs. Once, when Sir Ronald Storrs was governor in the 1920s, a team composed of Moslems, Christians, and Jews co-captained by Sergeant Schwili, a Jew, and P. C. Badawi, a Moslem, played on a barracks square until their lungs nearly burst. In modern Israel there were and are still Arab players, Israeli citizens, on the predominantly Jewish teams, and one Arab town, Bnei Sakhnin, with a team of its own in the league. Soccer remains a great and democratic leveler, but in the increasingly polarized communities of the Holy City in the late 1970s, it was no match for the demands of pious Jews.

The observant Ashkenazi Jews who increasingly congregated in the Katamon neighborhood pressured the municipality to shut down soccer at the local stadium, and in 1981 Hapoel moved to another field at the YMCA. Observant Jews were then able to take their Sabbath afternoon strolls without an accompaniment of yells and whistles, songs of adoration and abuse, the swell and sink of hope and disappointment. God was praised instead of goals.

Nobody I knew in Jerusalem could believe that I went to the

games, and in this respect I found myself in much the same situation as I had within my own soccer-phobic London family. Of course, what I really wanted to watch was English soccer, and from January to May 1978, while cataclysmic events unfolded around me—Anwar Sadat making peace with Menachem Begin, and so on—I bar-hopped in the hope of finding one establishment in the city enlightened enough to tune in to a channel showing European soccer, but no luck.

As for playing, there didn't seem to be much opportunity, and I didn't know where to look, and so, like the Jews in Moscow who had become Russian Orthodox priests because their spiritual needs had to be met *somehow*, I tried a different sport. A guy who lived near me, Yossi who ran the Little Souperie, got me involved in a pickup basketball game, but I was so useless that the other players on my team quickly lost patience, and it became clear that I should not think about coming back for a second go-round.

It was around this time that I began to lose interest in Hapoel—it was just too lonely there on the half-empty terraces—and I became involved, like everyone else in Israel, in the success of the Maccabi Tel Aviv basketball team that, with its six-foot-ten African-American star center, Aulcie Perry, was in contention for the 1978 European championship. After Maccabi's triumph and the delirium that followed, Aulcie Perry converted to Judaism, married a Yemenite-Israeli girl, and became, without a doubt, more popular than Prime Minister Begin. Unfortunately, a few years after his glory days on the basketball court were over, and at a point in his life when, by outward appearance, he seemed to have found both comfort and joy, Aulcie was arrested for trying to smuggle heroin into the U.S. and distribute it there. He served half of his ten-year sentence and returned to Israel to manage a burger joint.

Second Half

Chapter 12

E leni married John a few months after returning to England and I was happy for her. At first though I was lonely, drinking too much and writing a series of dismal poems. I sat at my desk and watched the blue jays swoop in and out of the trees outside my window. I had no family in Israel and the woman I had lived with since I was twenty-one was no longer around. "When we leave each other," the Danish poet Henrik Nordbrandt writes "we also leave all the places we have been together" and that is how I felt: our workman's house in Wivenhoe; a hotel in Heraklion, Crete where we spent a week on vacation and were greeted every morning by the din of pneumatic drills breaking concrete beneath our window; a cottage in Skibereen, Cork with pink fuchsia in its front garden and steaming cow pats in the sloping field at the back; a house on an estate near the lock in the Oxfordshire village of Iffley, married accommodation for graduate students of the university which we had lied to secure only to discover that, like us, all the tenants were single.

In the year that followed Eleni's departure I had quite a few very nice girlfriends, although I was never quite sure if they were more attracted to me or to my apartment. Talia was the slightly out-of-control daughter of an American rabbi (she smoked a lot of dope); Ada was a teacher in an experimental school; Orna and Liat were students at the art school; Edna had grown up on a kibbutz; Tami was a dancer who also happened to double as my cleaning lady; Ruth was a journalist from San Francisco; and Robyn was someone else's girlfriend, passing through.

In my memory of that time and the years that followed between Anwar Sadat's breakthrough visit to the Knesset (the Israeli house of representatives) in 1977 and the violence that erupted on Israel's northern border in July 1981, Jerusalem exists in some eternal naïve summer unsullied by politics. There, in that place, inhabited by someone in his mid-to-late twenties, not altogether a fool and not altogether wise, and with love, sex, poetry, and soccer on his mind, conflict is buried under bushes overgrown with wild honeysuckle and jasmine bursting like tiny stars at dusk. I barely sensed the seething disquiet of the Palestinians in East Jerusalem.

I met Sherry, my wife-to-be, at a wild party in the Jewish Quarter of the Old City, an area which, in the late 1970s, was very briefly home to a bohemian world of writers, painters (like Sherry), and photographers. I thought she was seventeen, but as it turned out I was a decade short, which was good news for me, as I was captivated from the start. We went up to the roof of the party house that offered a spectacular view of the Dome of the Rock, the Al-Aqsa Mosque, and the Western Wall. In moonlight that bathed everything in a surreal glow, I slowly became aware that our host's roof garden featured the kind of leafy potted plants that are frequently exchanged for large amounts of cash. In those years the Old City was home to all manner of unholy activities, though conducted under a broad spiritual canopy that covered even nonbelievers. The Sabbath atmosphere, for example, got to me every time.

Sherry, who looked like Molly Ringwald in *Sixteen Candles* five years before anyone knew what Molly Ringwald looked like, rented a tiny house on three levels, which were no more than three shelves really, on a narrow alleyway behind Misgav Ladach Street in the Jewish Quarter. The owner of the house, Harlap, a photographer, had moved on in search of a more spacious darkroom. If you came out through the gate and turned right, you were quickly on the Street of Chains and the tumult of the Shuk, the largest market in East Jerusalem; turn left and you would arrive at the stairway to a coffee shop with a balcony that overlooked the Kidron Valley. By ten in the morning one or two writers were already in their seats scribbling away.

Sherry had recently arrived from New York. By night she taught sculpture at a campus extension of the Bezalel art school in an old factory building near the Egged bus station, and by day she worked on her own canvases and paper, constructing a series of works that were charcoal marks on a black background, with a bit of white showing through. The white came from price tags borrowed from her other part-time job, which was selling local artifacts and craftwork at Charlotte's, a little store located behind the main Jerusalem post office.

Once we began to see each other, I abandoned my bicycle and we walked back and forth from Sherry's place to mine: from the omphalos of the Old City to that of the new. We'd go to the movies at the Orgil or the Orna on Hillel Street, or the Edson or Smadar, or most frequently the Cinematheque then located in Beit Agron building. If you were in your twenties, the Cinematheque was *the* place to be on Friday afternoon. There was a two o'clock movie that functioned as a kind of afternoon service, an art fix, for Jerusalem's secular neo-hippie community.

"It started like this," writes Yehuda Amichai, the greatest of all love-and-Jerusalem poets, "In the heart it became loose and easy and happy, as when someone feels his bootlaces loosening a bit." This is how it was. I lay on the top shelf of Sherry's house and read while she painted on the bottom level. We ate salads with Russian dressing straight out of the bowl, and we shared a fork. We drank cheap wine and 777 brandy that burned our throats. Except for when one of us went to teach, we were hardly apart. I wrote a poem about our life in the Old City shelves and it turned out to be the first piece of either poetry or fiction that I ever sold and published, in this case to *Stand* magazine in England. I was paid eleven pounds. I was so excited that, when my check arrived, I forgot to cash it.

My new, all-consuming relationship meant severing some old ties and associations. Soccer, of course, was already out of the window but for several months, before meeting Sherry, I had spent most of my nights bar-hopping, usually with Carmi but sometimes with Tomas Kulka, the Czech philosopher and my old friend from Kibbutz Lehavot Haviva. He too was now teaching at Hebrew University. We were all resident boozers in the garden of the Artists' House. More than a few times, Carmi and I, having exhausted the talk and company at the Piano Bar on Bezalel Street, The Khan near the railway station, Fink's, or the Artists' House, wound up toward dawn in a two-table drinker's café in Mahane Yehuda, the main West Jerusalem market. There we downed a last whiskey and watched the trucks unload their produce. The sun rose watercolor pink and stained the crates of parsley and cucumbers. I never tired of Carmi's wit and erudition, but when love announces itself with a trumpet blare, even the most fascinating of companions must become a bit player.

Now that I think of it, love came to Sherry and me with a

soundtrack: on the night we met, Van Morrison on the stereo in and out of the mystic, then Warren Zevon singing "Werewolves of London," and finally, while we were on the roof, Tom Waits rasping about a grapefruit moon and one star shining. In the nights that followed, an accompaniment of sometimes jarring, sometimes melodious sounds poured through the open window onto the top shelf of her house: prayers from the Wall, cries from the muezzin, late-night lovers in rooms with open windows also calling out to God, wailing cats, braying donkeys. On Friday mornings we walked to Nachlaot, a locality with tiny, makeshift houses that looked as if they had been thrown together from sheets, towels, and cardboard. There, in a hot corner bakery, two men wrapped dough around the surface of small round cushions before slapping it on the wall of an open concave oven. When they peeled off the oversized pita and handed it to you, it might have been nectar that they were passing along. Equally ambrosial was the challah from Menachem's on Bethlehem Street.

In September 1979, we moved in together, to an apartment at 4 Barak Street in Baka, a neighborhood that was at least a decade away from gentrification. I liked to walk alongside the nearby abandoned train track that had once stretched all the way from Jerusalem to Cairo. The number of discarded objects made the area look like a playground for Josef Beuys but wild poppies grew between the rails and wooden sleepers. Jerusalem always surprised me with what Saul Bellow once called "unexpected intrusions of beauty." Years later I sent Archie Rawlins, the hero of my novel *The Hiding Room*, down this railway line.

I bought a car, a Citroen GS with a pneumatic system that pumped up its front, then reared like a bucking bronco when you started it up. The neighborhood kids would come out to watch the show.

* * *

"Don't get married," Lea, my shrink, told me, "You're not ready." A week after offering me this piece of advice, *she* got married, only to have her union fall apart within a year. It was spring, my mother came to visit Jerusalem and behaved badly in characteristic fashion; "dark, horrible, disgusting place," she said when I drove her into the Old City and showed her the graceful Armenian arch that vaulted across the sky into the side of a church, "reminds of that horrible railway bridge on Park Avenue North" (she was talking about Willesden). Sherry, a kind-hearted person, tried her best with my mother, but she couldn't win. It is true that she was Jewish but the fact of the matter was that Doris couldn't really like any of her son's wives or potential wives. "Is she a games girl?" my mother asked me about Sherry, testing against some approval matrix circa 1927. "Does she play tennis?"

"She was a swimming champion," I replied, "All state, Massachusetts." It wasn't true, and Sherry had many accomplishments that I might have listed but I knew that whatever I said I wouldn't be able to make an impression. On a visit to Sherry's older sister Marsha, who lived in the Jewish Quarter of the Old City, my mother managed to make a scene, crying quietly then noisily on the sofa because we had been late picking her up at her hotel and for other reasons that remained indeterminate for several hours and which turned out to involve imagined slights that had supposedly occurred over the previous days.

We drove to Tel Aviv and brought her to restaurant in Jaffa that overlooked the Mediterranean. The sun was high, the sea calm, a few small boats dotted the harbor, it was an idyllic scene, but the menu proved a challenge. My mother wanted fish and what was on offer appeared exotic, or worse, Christian.

134

"St. Peter's Fish" was a speciality of the house, and Doris found the name offensive. "Don't they have a nice piece of plaice?" she asked me, "Or cod?" She was a wonderfully unreconstructed Londoner.

In the summer of 1980, I married Sherry. The wedding was in Newton, Mass. in a tent in Sherry's parents' back yard. We flew back to the States two weeks before the event and returned to Israel not long after. Shortly before the ceremony the rabbi, Richard Yellin, young, blue-eyed, reactionary, took me aside to ask if I knew what it symbolized when the groom broke the glass with a stamp of his foot. "Well," I said, "considering all the embarrassment and anxiety that surrounds the action and the jubilation and relief when the glass pops I'm assuming it has something to do with the tearing of the hymen."

"There's no need to use language like that," the rabbi replied, before setting me straight. It was a hot August day and a great party. People danced and got drunk; my best man, Barak Berkowitz, made a lovely speech, something about Adam, the Garden of Eden, and the breezy time of day; the Bo Winaker band played songs by Billy Joel, ignoring our request for Eric Clapton (but that didn't matter); even my mother, who had come with the rest of my immediate family, brothers and their wives, nieces and nephews, managed to limit her complaints to a solitary grumble that Sherry's father wasn't asking her to dance. At some point my nephew James, Geoffrey's oldest son and closer to me in age than my brother, burned his hand in water from the Instant Hot tap in the kitchen, my friend Yale Barash threw up and Sherry got a migraine from the camera flashes. In other words, it was a wedding.

We did find time for a brief honeymoon in Vermont. Sherry hadn't seen her younger sister Suzie for a year and so she invited her along with her boyfriend (later husband) Jonathan. I wasn't too happy about this, especially when it turned out that they didn't have any money on them and we all had to share a motel room with two double beds. We watched the U.S. Tennis Open together and then went bowling. I scored a career high 186.

We returned to Israel and our apartment in Baka; it was spacious enough for both a small studio for Sherry and a study for me. The bed, much to Sherry's father's consternation when he visited from Boston, was the first thing you saw when you entered the apartment. He sat gingerly on its edge and told us in somewhat disappointed terms that we lived in a slum.

The painter Michael Kovner, his wife Mimi, and their two sons occupied the apartment downstairs. Sometimes Michael's father, Abba, the renowned poet, came to visit with Michael's mother. The documentary *Partisans of Vilna* recounts the Kovners' extraordinary bravery during World War II. At the Eichmann trial, Abba testified in a white suit, as if for the Day of Atonement.

There were three other families in the old house, and our ground-floor neighbors, Pirke and Yigal, cultivated a beautiful garden with a lemon tree at its center. Our laundry, hung out in the sun to dry, was forever falling from our line into the branches of the tree that, as we made only sporadic collections, would look for days as if it had grown clothes instead of fruit. Our next-door neighbors, Munie and Ronit, grew freesias on their patio in abandoned white enamel sinks they had found by the railway line.

On the road to Tel Aviv when we drove to the beach there was sometimes a great fragrant bang of orange blossom that penetrated the windows of our car. But despite the sensual orchards and the pull of the shore and the warm Mediterranean sea, I always breathed a sigh of relief when, on the way home, the car began its ascent to Jerusalem after crossing the intersection at Sh'aar Hagai. I wanted old stone and cool nights. God, it was said, gave ten parts of beauty to the world, and nine of them he gave to Jerusalem. I could believe that, just as I could believe that he had given nine of the world's ten parts of trouble to the same place.

* * *

I was still officially a student at Oxford, not resident, but none-theless completing my D.Phil. Almost a year after we moved to Baka, I received notification that my supervisor, Larzer Ziff, had returned to the States to take up a position at Johns Hopkins. The university appointed Dr. Weaver, an Englishman this time, to oversee my thesis. We corresponded. It was clear from the beginning that he didn't like the way I was approaching my topic, which had condensed to a study of the novels of Saul Bellow. Unfortunately, according to Dr. Weaver, I had developed "an American style" in both my writing and my thinking. I returned to England on a visit and tried to sort things out.

It was early summer, and Oxford was in picture-postcard state: deer grazed in Magdalen College gardens, and students punted leisurely down the river. I knew these seductions very well, and if I hadn't been inoculated against them first by the hurly-burly of New York and then by the sensory delights of Jerusalem, I might have succumbed. Dr. Weaver was ensconced in Professor Ziff's old room. I sat down. We talked for a while. He described the ways in which he wanted me to alter the direction of my thesis and explained how to go about doing so. I was feeling very hip and foreign, wised-up and on the ball, much too full of myself.

"It seems to me," I said, when he had finished, "that you want me to surround my thesis with bullshit."

"What you call 'bullshit,' Mr. Wilson," Weaver replied, "we call scholarship."

I understood that this was the end of my English education.

Back in Jerusalem I transferred my thesis to the Hebrew University, and it is from there, the institution founded by Albert Einstein, that I eventually secured my degree. For the next year, because of both our art school and Carmi connections, Sherry and I moved in what were, for us, lofty circles. Ambitious beginners in the world of art and literature, we were in awe both of the permanent residents and the visiting greats who blew through town. We met Jim Dine, John Updike, Stanley Kunitz and his wife, the painter Elise Asher and, largely through Carmi, a number of other visiting poets: Dannie Abse, Jon Silkin, and Henrik Nordbrandt. There was also Rita Dove, then a little-known African-American poet. Rita, along with her husband Fred Viebahn, was an annual visitor to Jerusalem for a while. They were a much sought-after couple on the social scene: not many black writers visited Jerusalem, and even fewer who were married to Germans with shoulder-length blond hair.

What drew those writers and artists who were not put off by the politics to Jerusalem was, I think, the city's heady mix of the old and the new, its physical beauty, and the exhilarating sense of being in a great spiritual capital of the world at a moment when it was bursting with secular creative ideas. This was six years before the first intifada, before attitudes both inside Israel and around the globe hardened and Jerusalem received as many cancellations as visits from its ambivalent invitees.

But soon, too soon, Jerusalem began to change. The movie

theaters moved out of the center of town into strip malls. Some of the bars closed. You could feel the stirrings of resentment in the Old City, and by 1981 Jews rarely wandered until two or three in the morning in the Moslem Quarter, as we had, peering down alleyways where small braziers glowed and a burnt orange light from the fires illuminated vats of sesame oil. Even the Cinematheque found a new appointment on Derech Hebron Street overlooking the Valley of Hinnom.

For four years I had been ardently in love with Jerusalem, in love with its noise and its silence, its electric and daunting politics, the sensual overload that it offered every day: scents, colors, visions. We had great friends and great conversations. I tried to speak Hebrew but whenever I did so I was asked to speak English because "Your Hebrew is terrible." On Fridays I did my chores and rounds like everyone else: mopped the tiled floor, visited the market to bargain over vegetables, meats, and spices, bought challah at the bakery, then flowers from the guy who stood on the corner near my shrink's office on Ramban Street. My Jerusalem shopping and walking credentials were in order. The lilac heart of the city intoxicated me even when explosions rocked it. I knew that what I was experiencing were the last great hours of rock-and-roll love in all the quarters and neighborhoods of the city, its secrets locked in the crevices of their walls, all manner of desire, prayer, and yearning. There are stones that want to burst the heart.

My wife, in white on the night that I met her, dressed like the young girls who, according to tradition, danced in the fields outside the walls of Jerusalem on Tu B'Av (a kind of ancient Israeli Valentine's Day, and the beginning of the grape harvest) in the glow of a full summer moon. The day after the party, I'd discovered Sherry in her neighbor's front yard. She had stirred henna and tea in boiling water and painted the mixture onto her hair before applying tinfoil and stretching out in the hot sun. The end result was red, red, red, like everything that burned between us that day.

In Jerusalem, even more so than in New York, all the anxieties of a self-effacing English Jew had fallen away from me. The knife flash from Gladstone Park, the JEW inscribed on the back of my anorak, were no more than raindrops on Freud's windshield. Aside from my Hebrew language problem (and Sherry was equally deficient in that regard), I felt very much at home. Sherry, I know, felt the same way. So, naturally, we left.

Chapter 13

We moved to Boston at the beginning of summer in 1981. Sherry was pregnant with our son Adam, conceived in the Holy City, and I had secured a job teaching part-time in the English Department at Tufts University. We decided to rent an apartment on Hanover Street in Little Italy; we wanted to be near an outdoor market—Haymarket was close by—and also, I suppose, we still yearned to reside in a neighborhood where English wasn't necessarily the first language. It made us feel that we hadn't quite left Jerusalem.

We lived above Mama Cantina's restaurant, and our windows overlooked the Peace Garden of St. Leonard's Church. The scents of cooking, especially garlic, wafted in, not only from below but also from the apartment next door, where our octogenarian landlady Mrs. Pagliucci lived. When I walked down the street to take the T to work, the Italian owner of a children's shoe store who liked to hang out in his doorway would say to me, "Bonjourno Professore." I loved it. The whole street seemed to go black and white as he spoke, and I might have been crossing in front of Rome's Trevi fountain. When Adam was born on March 25, 1982, he became the first Jewish baby to have a *brit* on

Hanover Street for about half a century.

Italians, including some Italian-Americans, love soccer, and I was happy to discover that the walls of Caffe Dello Sport, a few doors down from our apartment building, were decorated with team shots of the great World Cup-winning Italian teams, known as the Azzurri, and their stars. I didn't know it at the time, but Caffe Dello Sport was also a popular spot for local mobsters—they had a back room all to themselves. Or at least they thought it was all to themselves; it turned out that the FBI was bugging the place. Not long after we moved in, someone got shot in the pizza place on the other side of the street. The victim was a young man, a local nuisance, who had deviated from certain unwritten neighborhood rules. Caffe Dello Sport seemed particularly lively that day.

The 1982 World Cup was played in Spain, but dispiritingly none of the games, except for the final, were broadcast on U.S. TV. In order to watch it, I had to go to the Bradford, a seedy hotel in downtown Boston, not far from the area known as the Combat Zone, which featured the city's most notorious strip clubs. The matches were shown on closed-circuit TV and projected onto a large screen set up in a dismal oak-paneled ballroom. I didn't know anyone in the sparse audience, and I made no connections. The experience was depressing but I continued to go, drawn by forces that were by now so immured in my being that I was hardly able to reflect upon them. Soccer had always been where I went to escape from loneliness, but in Boston it reinforced it. Sherry was busy with the baby (as was I), but I had made few new friends in Boston, and Little Italy, while delightful in appearance and ambience, was a closed society.

Sherry and I had met in between World Cups, and she was mildly disturbed to discover my addiction, and baffled that I simply *had* to head off for the Bradford every morning or afternoon, which was afternoon or evening in Spain. I think, postpartum, she suspected my real destination was The Naked I. At some point she claimed that I had tricked her in Israel by not revealing the depths of my obsession with soccer. "Passion," I said, "not obsession. And in any case, there is no soccer here."

On the morning of the World Cup final between Italy and West Germany, I wheeled Adam in his stroller to the open market and stood in the penumbra of various stalls, testing, tasting, and purchasing the abundant miracles of American produce on display: fruits, vegetables, bread, cheese, wine, oysters shucked on the spot, strawberries as big as tomatoes. I breathed in the salt air off the ocean and felt refreshed, but I missed Jerusalem. There were no vivid spice stalls in Boston, no embroidered dresses, miniature drums, or pungent untreated sheepskin jackets for sale. I missed the Middle Eastern bazaar of the Old City. On the other hand, in Haymarket I didn't feel like an interloper: a customer from the wrong side of the East-West Jerusalem divide tolerated out of necessity. After an hour or so, we came back down Hanover Street, past Mike's Pastry with its extravagant multilayered cakes, past the overweight guys who hung out on street corners and watched to make sure that vehicles belonging to their double-parked superiors remained unticketed, past the numerous cafes and restaurants serving pizza, pasta, and cannoli. There were a few more Italian flags than usual on display, but no bunting, and no sense of drama to come.

Italy won the World Cup by beating West Germany 3–1. In Toronto, a North American city not *that* far way, 300,000 people poured into the streets to rejoice in the Azzurri. By contrast, the celebrations on Hanover Street were desultory, and nothing compared to what happened there when Italy beat France in the infamous Zinedine Zidane head-butt final of 2006. Then the street was thronged with celebrating Italian-Americans, which demonstrates just how far soccer progressed in the national U.S. consciousness in the intervening twenty-four years. I watched the 1982 party, such as it was, through the window of my study. Adam was asleep in his crib.

* * *

In the fall we moved to a larger rental in Cambridge: an old Victorian house on Mount Pleasant Street. Through a friend, I found a pickup game to play in—it was co-ed, a first for me. The group was organized by a soccer-obsessed American photographer, Jim Dow, who taught at the Museum School. Jim wore English club shirts to every game; his favorite was the claret and blue of West Ham. He had made a pilgrimage to the U.K. in order to take pictures of its soccer stadiums: empty, haunted, and magnificent. There were three or four of us from England and Ireland in the game, and we clearly had the hardest time adjusting to the uncompetitive and good-natured spirit that presided. We had been brought up to be ruthless in soccer and didn't know any other way to play. My friend Peter Rhodes was an equal opportunity shin-kicker, he had been hard-tackling everyone who got in his way for twenty years and he simply couldn't put the brakes on. An American playing basketball in the U.K. would, I'm sure, experience the same difficulty in modifying his or her activity. The game was a superb ego boost for me and the other foreigners: the Americans on the team had no idea of our true level in the larger world of soccer, and thought we were fantastic. We were intramural at best, but to them, we were semipro.

A couple of months after Adam's first birthday, I sprained my ankle lunging for the ball. The result was six weeks of cast and crutches. In the middle of this period we went to England to show my mother her new grandson. On the plane I took a couple of Percocet, and that is probably why I removed someone else's luggage from the belt and transported it in a taxi all the way to North West London. "Football!" my mother said in her front hall, after taking in my cast and learning about the errant bags. "It's all because of football. Everything he does is because of football."

Chapter 14

When our son Gabriel was born in November 1985, we bought a house in Newton, Mass. There, a few months after settling in, I learned what was required of a suburban parent and began my life as a coach.

For a period that spanned the next fourteen years and ran always from September through June, I devoted a considerable number of hours to offering an admittedly quirky, English-tinged, amateurish brand of soccer instruction to boys, and a few girls, aged 5–15. I also assistant-assistant-coached baseball, a sport of which, as previously mentioned, I knew almost nothing. Adam played soccer in a K-1 program but baseball was always his first love; for Gabe, when his time came, soccer was in the ascendancy.

During the peak sporting months of April to June, when baseball overlapped with soccer, I put in about sixteen to eighteen hours a week either coaching games or watching my sons hit, catch, or kick a ball. My spectator hours were shorter during the dark winter months when only basketball and hockey were in progress, but not by much. Hockey, in particular, was a time-consuming occupation, wherein lacing a single skate at five a.m.

in a freezing rink could easily take twenty minutes.

I'm not including in this estimate time spent in the following ways: purchasing and upgrading footwear, outfits, and equipment; collecting and dropping off kids whose parents had real jobs and were busy working; at organizational meetings; on confirmatory phone calls with other coaches; engaged in exchanges of varying intensity with parents who were happy, sad, aggrieved, or worried about their kid's performances on the field; and in the pursuit ("You look." "I am looking!" "Well, look again." "I've been looking for half an hour!") of shin guards, protective cups, mitts, batting gloves, baseball bats, soccer balls that needed to be inflated, skates, shorts, helmets, and the eternally missing lids of plastic water flasks.

My situation was not, of course, unusual. I wasn't *that much* of a slave to my sons, and I hope, where soccer was concerned, I wasn't one of those frustrated egos indulging mega pro-coach fantasies on the sidelines. My reasons for getting involved were both thoughtless and exigent. Every year, millions of children participate in youth sports across America, and the number is growing; not everyone can spectate; and, as Bob Dylan pointed out a long time ago, everybody's got to serve somebody.

Coaching, at least in Newton, was, I soon learned, commonly regarded as both a civic duty and, once you'd got it, potentially a job for life. And while the post bestowed your own personal fiefdom, the elections were refreshingly democratic. You didn't actually have to be a parent, and you didn't have to be a guy. No stigma was attached to the boy who had a female coach, and when it came to leading the pint-size troops into battle, general aggressiveness, and cutthroat on-the-line decisions, the women, as far as I could tell, danced to the same drummer as the men. Most important, you didn't, unless you were in charge of one of the high-level "travel teams" that played other towns and cities outside Newton, need expertise in your chosen sport. In Little League, for example, I was an assistant to the assistant coach; my job was to keep players more or less in the region of the bench, be aware of who was on deck, and protect young heads from practice swings and foul balls. I wasn't alone in enjoying a vital but diminished status, enforced by my relative ignorance of baseball. With the rise of soccer as a participatory sport, there were legions of my American counterparts loose in the field. Schooled by monotonous videos, they patrolled the white lines bellowing happily ambiguous directions—"Switch fields!"—in full knowledge of their inability to approximate either the skills or the tactical know-how of their players.

The pleasure of coaching was not always apparent, either during practices or on game days, but for me now, after more than a decade in retirement from that particular parental exertion, they inhere in Proustian stubs of memory which I trip over while, let's say, staring out the window on a particularly lovely autumn afternoon that is charged with vibrant yellow and red leaves, now soaking in a sudden downpour. I recall a second-grade game on a sharp fall day when our six-year-old sweeper, Shane Toman—who, like half the team, was spacey, verging on permanent orbit—got paralyzed out of position somewhere near the center circle. "Get back, Shane!" I yelled. "Back near the goal!" Shane stayed rooted to the spot. The attackers from the other team lurched forward. I fell into silent despair, but then Shane's father, Art, a quiet graceful man who made violins for a living, yelled "The Little House, Shane, go near the Little House!" Shane clicked into high gear, sprinted down the field, and launched himself into a saving tackle.

Moments like that made up the undiluted good stuff, but there were also murkier incidents, which seem to capture in miniature both the high comedy and the furious desires that lie behind the drama of American parenting as it relates to sports. Little League Minors, late June 1992. I'm on the fourth tier of a weather-beaten stand, surveying the greensward of Richardson Field, the jewel in the crown of our neighborhoods' ballparks. It's high noon, the heat is sweltering, and there's a contest in progress between two teams already eliminated from the playoffs. Their coach wants our fattest player, George, the son of a Methodist minister, moved back off the plate because his stomach is obscuring the strike zone. Our coach: "Jesus Christ! Leave the kid alone!" Their coach: "Don't take the name of the Lord in vain." Our coach: "What are you, a fucking altar boy?" During pre-season training that year, Wally (our coach), had urged the nine-year-olds to watch *Bull Durham* in preparation for the season ahead ("You've all heard the word *fuck*, haven't you?"). He was immensely popular. Their coach approaches, with menace. "You," he says, "are a disgrace. You ought to be kicked out of the league." Wally strips off his yellow tank top, does a little Marquis of Queensberry tap dance, but then thinks better of it and picks up an aluminum baseball bat to swing at his adversary. It is clear now that he is drunk. The umpire, Lowball Larry, gets between the demon parent-coaches, and, after a tepid exchange of insults, the game resumes, with all the players tense and trembling.

I once coached in a game between seven-year-olds when my opposite number ran onto the field to protest one of the thirteen-year-old referee's decisions. For fifteen minutes, he ignored the child-ref's polite requests to leave the field; after he had been issued a yellow warning card and then a red expulsion card, there was a rain of insults from "our" parents directed at the obstructionist coach—including, "Get off the field, you putz!"

Eventually, the young referee walked off, got into the back of his mother's Volvo station wagon, and threatened to go home. When I approached the opposition parents and asked them to control their coach, they told me to fuck off.

When did the suburbs and the small towns of America go mad? It must have been when the Boomers came of age as parents, because the Boomers themselves generally produce nostalgic variations of "It wasn't like this in my day." The standard Edenic version in play for the last thirty years or so goes something like this: We went down after school/on weekends to the park/court/field; there were no parents around; we used sweaters for bases/goalposts; we organized ourselves and had fun; we played until it was dark, and the ball was a pale, spinning lozenge of love. I have made such claims myself.

Maybe I was jealous of all the parental attention lavished on my team. There were times in my childhood when I was desperate for some parental interference. Once, in Gladstone Park, a gang of kids with various makeshift weapons invaded a soccer game that I was playing in and tried to start a fight. My friend Barry Woodward's dad was a policeman and, as luck would have it, he happened to be standing not too far away, watching the game in progress with his leashed German shepherd sitting quietly next to him. David Stanley, who was sporting a knuckle-duster and who had just been released from juvie, punched Richard Eker in the face. And Mr. Woodward did absolutely nothing. He wanted to teach us that while we were children in age, we should not be so in protectedness. In the raw arena of the park, we had to learn how to defend ourselves. I felt betrayed by the entire adult world.

Boomers, as well as the helicopter parents that followed, have no one to blame but themselves for the increase in pressure on their children. We shadow and loom over them like the statuesque heads that dwarf the tiny figures in Watteau's paintings. This, for my peers, was a neat switch: our own parents, those much maligned, famously uptight "Greatest Generation" souls, were actually inclined to leave kids to their own devices. Of course, in the golden fifties and sixties, both England and America were imagined as safer. The park was for players, not perverts; parents didn't have to worry that their children would be stalked on their way to the soccer pitch or the rough baseball diamond between the trees. Those parents, in retrospect, now seem astonishingly laid-back.

The result of our current condition, as everyone knows, is that out on the playing fields and courts, kids are overprotected and their parents overinvolved. "The parents should leave at the gate," a fellow coach once told me. "We'd all be a lot happier." But they don't, and when I was in the role of parent, not coach, I didn't either.

Here's an example of my own stupidity: it was the last minor-league game of the 1991 season, and the Astros, Adam's team, needed to win in order to make the playoffs. Adam, an excellent all-around baseball player, was one of the team's good pitchers— in my opinion, he was the best—but he was not pitching that day. Throughout the game, I kept muttering to the father standing next to me behind the cage, "Why doesn't Wally put Adam in? Does he want to win this thing or what?" In the bottom of the sixth, the other team came up for their last at-bat; the score was an unlikely 3–2 in our favor. The pitcher walked the first two batters. Wally brought Adam in as a *closer*. I started to go nuts. "What's he doing?" I asked my companion. "Is Wally crazy, putting a nine-year-old kid in a situation like this? This is gonna destroy him!" The other dad replied dryly, "I thought you wanted your son out

151

there." In the gathering twilight, Adam gave up a run, got two outs, and then walked in the winning run. He tried to fight back tears. Out of the corner of my eye, I saw his mother enter the circle of gloom around the pitcher's mound to offer solace.

*   *   *

As the years and the seasons passed, I noticed a strange phenomenon with the smaller children. Well, perhaps it wasn't strange at all, but simply an intriguing extension of the self-esteem movement: talented players were never removed from basketball or baseball games when they performed well—only soccer. Somehow, youth soccer had morphed into a locus of anxiety and repressed competitive angst. Early on in my time as an American soccer coach, I had a boy on our team, Adam P., who could slalom past defenders as if they were flagpoles and score at will. His extraordinary six-year-old talent enraged all the parents on the sidelines (except his own), and every time he scored, there was a Greek chorus of "Take him out!" from the soccer moms and dads. A fairly new arrival from the unreconstructed United Kingdom via Israel (where they had other problems), I was loath to remove a striker who ensured a mammoth victory every time he got near the ball. Take him out? Why? He's a superstar. The answer, of course, was that everyone else's egos would collapse if Adam P. continued to perform as he was capable.

Once, on the butterfly morning of a tournament for nine-year-olds in which I was coaching a team, I was approached by a group of mothers who told me that they had "been up all night" trying to figure out our best lineup for the day. This was a cluster of four or five professional women, some of whom had not heard of soccer until their children had enrolled to play the sport a few weeks earlier. Suddenly, "fair play" was out the window and the knives were glinting—this was a tournament! Clearly I made the wrong coaching decisions because we lost in the semifinals. At day's end, slivers of orange peel in the sky, the up-all-night mothers walked past me in the car park. They got in their shiny automobiles, slammed doors, and sent me to Coventry. I suppose this should have given me some insight into what was coming down the road for my son Gabe, but at the time I simply thought their behavior was an aberration.

Then an incident occurred that altered my perspective entirely on suburban life and almost closed out my interest in coaching all together. Gabe was a wonderful soccer player: lithe, speedy, and skillful, with a ferocious shot. He had quickly been promoted to the Boston Area Youth Soccer League travel team for nine-years-olds and was one of its stars. In his second season, shortly after he turned ten, he began to develop a range of anxieties that were eventually diagnosed as obsessive-compulsive disorder. OCD, punch line of many jokes and throwaway remarks, is, in fact, a terribly hard and painful condition. Gabe's life was profoundly affected, and while he was (in a slow and difficult process of discovery and treatment) greatly helped by effective therapies and medication, he also had to endure some of the side effects of the latter. He put on some weight and as a result slowed down on the soccer field; he stopped to tie and untie his laces so he could check that either his mother or I were still standing on the sidelines. In short, at ten years old, he was not the player he had been.

His two coaches were both fathers of other boys on Newton's U11s. They wanted Gabe off their team; from their point of view, he had become a liability even as a substitute. But they knew he was suffering. Here's what they did. In previous years, at the midpoint of the season, during the winter break when the

153

weather grew cold, the team played for a few weeks in an indoor league. The coaches told Gabe (and Sherry and me) that this year there would be no indoor winter league. One night we took Gabe to a local indoor soccer facility where he wanted to watch a friend of his play in an intramural game. We arrived in the dark, and moved into the brightly lit arena. There, out on the artificial turf, were all Gabe's former teammates involved in a fast paced match against another town's team. The coaches only noticed us when the referee blew the final whistle. When I tried to talk to them, they hurried past us red-faced. One said "Hi Gabe." His former teammates, who had clearly been asked to keep Gabe in the dark about his impending winter isolation and banishment from U11 soccer, rushed away sheepish and confused. My son, then as now, possessed an extraordinary courage. He cried, but not for long. It wasn't long before he was back on track in soccer, but later in life he took up boxing.

*   *   *

In "Of the Affection of Fathers to Their Children," Montaigne argues that parental latitude is preferable to tight-fisted control. As parents, like it or not, we are inevitably consumed by jealousy and envy of our children for the simple reason that, all things going as nature intended, we shall die before them. For Montaigne, true affection means letting go of this envy which so frequently, in contemporary America anyway, with its Puritan tradition, finds its justification in the supposedly educative importance of a child's earning his or her own way. Since the 1980s, however, a large segment of Boomer and post-Boomer helicopter parents has been fixated on a quite different form of control, one motivated by terminal narcissism. They want to make sure that their kids get into the best colleges, and part of this process involves their child's belonging to a successful sports team from an early age. I often sensed that for a disturbingly high percentage of parents in my city, no victories for Newton's U11s translated to no Harvard down the line.

In fact, after a few years of coaching, I began to think that, for the most part, my own childhood soccer experience, almost completely free of parental observation, had not been sad at all, but highly desirable. My sons and their friends played on grass that was green and mown, on teams where everyone owned their own ball, and wore designer cleats and spotless uniforms with names and numbers on the back of their shirts. At the early stages, K–5, they were awarded gleaming trophies simply for participation. If you had told me about this soccer nirvana as a child, I would have been full of envy. On the other hand, the thought of my own or my friends' parents running my soccer life would have seemed both absurd and highly undesirable.

Once, when I was still Gabe's coach, some mothers reported me to the local soccer board for abandoning a training session during a torrential rainstorm. "How," they wanted to know, "could the team be expected to bond" if I cancelled practice? Practice, that endless tedium of unwanted instruction ("Everybody in a line!"), is much valued by the parent community, which has a naïve faith in its ability to translate its children's raw energy into manifestations of Olympian grace. There is also a resilient belief in America that talent can be taught. My worst moments in coaching involved enduring parental criticism of the length, frequency, and instructional content of my team practices. There's a reason why the kids always implore the coach, "Can't we just play?" They want to experience the Big Garden that I once knew—the clear, unimpeded thrill of a pickup game, where breaks are impromptu and there's room for all manner of invention and foolishness. It's liberating when no one barks "Keep your head in there," or audibly groans when you make a mistake, or presses a large red face to yours and roars, "Are you having fun?" Once, I arrived at a baseball game in time to hear a coach announce, "And no singing on the bench." In an ideal world, the coach, like Marx's state, should wither away.

But then, what would I have done with my Saturdays? I would have had to relinquish those moments of coaching that don't arise from stirring victories or brave defeats, but transpire in incongruous and unpredictable and oddly touching exchanges between the coach and his or her wards. What I prefer to remember are the thank-you cards signed by everyone at season's end, and the epiphanies, my kneeling in a sudden downpour to untie, then retie, seven-year-old Alex Bullit's rain-sodden laces—and all the while him patting me very gently on the head as if to say, "Good dog."

From time to time, I run into young men in their twenties whom I coached when they were kids. One of them, Brian Colony-Roiter, is presently a Buddhist monk in India. Brian liked to play fullback mainly because he enjoyed taking goal kicks. For a decade, I recommended that he direct his kicks to the side of the pitch and whack the ball as far up in that angled direction as he could get it. He preferred however to slam the ball down the middle, usually in a direct line to the feet of our opponent's most skilled and cultivated striker. I guess he was after a challenge. As it happens, Brian turned up as a student at Tufts. In his freshman year he came to see me: he wanted course recommendations. I refused to give him any. When had he ever taken my advice? I see him now, robed and shaved, like the young soccer-obsessed Tibetan monks in the movie *The Cup*, dribbling through the foothills of the Himalayas: prayer, discipline, tradition … Soccer!

Chapter 15

In January 1993, I published a short story, "Bank Holiday," in *The New Yorker*, my first in that magazine. My father-in-law, Louis Kaitz, who ran a lumber company, said, "That could lead to something." I thought it *was* something, but in a way he was right. What it led to was more fiction and some nonfiction assignments. One of my articles resulted in a run-in with my congressman, Barney Frank. I had portrayed him in what I thought were glowing terms as broad-minded, tolerant, and not afraid to take on a particular branch of government, the INS, which I had personally witnessed harassing green card holders while they were trying to pass their citizenship tests. But Barney took exception to my description of him as wearing a jogging suit and "panting" when I had run into him at a local coffee shop. He claimed that he didn't own a jogging suit and never panted in public places. He sent the magazine's editors three screeds on congressional notepaper. I had only recently become an American citizen, and it was unnerving to have my new representative turn against me in this way. In one bitter moment, Barney expressed the wish that I had remained singularly British. Barney had a lot of enemies. I couldn't figure out why I was now one of them. I guess he was sensitive about his weight.

In one "Shouts and Murmurs" column, I wrote about seeking out a pub in Brighton, Mass., in order to watch English soccer on satellite TV. Soccer was beginning to get some purchase in the U.S., as the World Cup was scheduled to take place there the following summer, but there were no Americans in The Blind Pig, the bar that I visited. Instead, the place was packed with Irishmen who were having a great time teasing the few Englishmen who had joined the crowd. The game in progress was an FA Cup final between Tottenham and Nottingham Forest. I had my Spurs shirt on. An Arsenal supporter who was standing behind me said, "Take that fucking shirt off before I burn it," but before he had a chance to strike a match, Spurs scored, after the ball seemed to have deflected into the net off a player's backside. "You think that's impressive?" the Irish guy standing next to me, who later claimed he had once been a jockey, said. "I once scored a goal with my dick." Things continued in this vein for the entire ninety minutes of play.

During halftime, there was an animated discussion about the forthcoming World Cup USA. Would it be a blessing or a curse? The bulk of largely inebriated opinion, including my own, inclined toward disaster. There were already rumors that the U.S. soccer authorities and the TV people both were pressing FIFA (the Federation Internationale de Football, soccer's governing body) to change the rules to make the game more exciting for American fans and more available to commercials: bigger goals, quarters instead of halves. Americans, we all agreed, didn't *understand* soccer. They loved "pitchers' duels" in baseball that ended in 1–0 victories for one side or the other, but whined ceaselessly about "low-scoring" soccer games. American sports were all stop-start, usually with breaks taken for a small white man to tell large black men what to do. Soccer was free-flowing, endlessly fluid, and inventive. Who on earth had made the decision to hold the World Cup in the only country *on the entire globe* that didn't care about it?

This general estimation was reinforced for me two months later when, on June 9, 1993, during a summer downpour at Foxboro Stadium, in Massachusetts, I watched the United States, playing its penultimate game in the dreary, irrelevant U.S. Cup, score two goals to defeat and humiliate a shabby, inept England team. Near the end of the game, the phalanx of England supporters grouped behind me in the stands had lowered their red and white St. George's-cross flags and chanted, "We're such shit it's unbelievable!" In England, self-derision and hooliganism often run hand-in-hand, so I feared the worst, but to my surprise the visiting hooli-fans good-humoredly (England had not yet been eliminated from the World Cup in the qualifying rounds) broke into "U.S.A., give us a song!"

How would the local crowd respond? I looked around: everywhere I turned, there seemed to be large groups of under-fourteen girls' teams, all proudly sporting their uniforms and sitting in neat lines bookended by their chaperone coaches. A weak and unimaginative "U.S.A.!" chant wafted across the field and died. Somewhere around the center circle, an England midfield player performed an athletically spectacular but, in soccer terms, utterly inconsequential maneuver. The England fans barely noticed; the rest of the crowd went wild. Oh, Jesus, I thought, the Irish guys in the pub were right. Why did FIFA ever let America have the World Cup? The women's World Cup—fine. But the *real* World Cup, with Romario and Bebetto and that artful ponytailed Italian-Buddhist Roberto Baggio? Forget it. It's never going to work.

∗   ∗   ∗

This bleak assessment didn't stop me from suggesting to Tina Brown that she let me cover the World Cup for *The New Yorker*. At the time she had someone else in mind for the job, Salman Rushdie, but in December 1993, before the final draw had even taken place in Las Vegas, the *fatwa* on Salman Rushdie's life had yet to be lifted (officially it still has not), and it quickly became clear that the security measures necessary to get him from venue to venue and in and out of the press box at matches across America would be an insurmountable obstacle to his taking the gig.

And so, with Christmas approaching, I found myself at Caesar's Palace in Las Vegas, caucusing with various members of the unreconstructed British press instead of the polite and tolerant Americans because I couldn't pass up an opportunity to sit next to one of my childhood heroes, Brian Glanville. Glanville, then in his sixties, was the author of the YA novel *Goalkeepers Are Crazy*, which I had loved when I was ten (and still do), along with numerous seminal pieces on soccer for various British broadsheets and tabloids. He was the doyen of British soccer journalists, a man whose word was gold.

When it was time for the ceremony to commence, Dick Clark came onstage to announce that the draw we were about to witness was "more than just a show," and in fact constituted a bonafide "historic occasion"; then Barry Manilow sang. Sepp Blatter, the diminutive, unctuous, and much-loathed (to this day) general secretary of FIFA, arrived to explain the way in which the draw had been seeded. He beckoned Faye Dunaway from the wings and, in what the British reporter next to me described as "a truly nauseating moment," bowed and appeared to kiss her hand, saying, "May I call you Faye?" and then, "Would you enjoy if I offer you the official ball?"

Not long after, Michelle Akers-Stahl, then captain of the world champion United States Women's National Team, came onstage to help pluck Ping-Pong balls from goldfish bowls to determine when and where the teams would be playing. At this point, Glanville turned to me and asked, "Who the fuck is that?" And when I told him he replied, "Well what the fuck is *she* doing up there?"

Evenings in Las Vegas with the soccer cognoscenti of the world, journalism division: a mole-dark sky breached by a hundred thousand lights. In the casinos, minds cratered deep into slots and numbers, and on the edge of the city, ochre sands where you might hallucinate a crocodile sliding after great translucent fish.

On the night following the draw, I went for dinner with the Italian journalist Anna DiLellio who, in the time-honored fashion of journalists interviewing other journalists when no one else is available, had selected Glanville and myself earlier in the day. We decided to eat at the Luxor, the pyramid-shaped casino with a hologram Sphinx guarding its entrance. It was said that savvy gamblers avoided the Luxor, as its owners had filled the hotel's basement with genuine Egyptian artifacts from the time of the pharaohs, and everyone knew that you shouldn't mess around with objects destined for the Egyptian afterlife. If proof was needed, a construction worker had been killed in 1992 during the construction of this Nevada pyramid, a victim of the angry gods.

Anna DiLellio was covering the Cup for *L'Independente*. It was her first (and last) venture into sports journalism. A sociologist by training—she was teaching at Sarah Lawrence and finishing her Ph.D. at Columbia—Anna was also the Italian newspaper's New

York correspondent on politics and culture. It became increasingly clear to me as the Cup progressed that all kinds of people had been pressed into service to write about soccer because there weren't that many individuals living in the U.S. and regularly employed by the American media who knew anything about it. (Seven months hence, at the Brazil v USA game in the Rose Bowl, I met an English guy who was reporting on the games for the Pasadena affiliate of NBC radio. "How long have you worked for the network?" I asked. "I don't," he replied, "I'm their L.A. accountant.")

We eschewed the Pyramid Café and took the elevator up to a Nile-themed restaurant that served various "Egyptian" delights. In a stroke of multicultural genius, the dessert menu was headed "Elysian Fields." Over "Nubian" burgers, Anna told me she would be writing about disagreements that might arise between players and managers, injuries, fans, and that she planned to conduct some post-game locker room interviews. The games themselves would be covered by the sports editor of *L'Independente*, who would fly in come June. I asked about her soccer affiliation. She said, "When I was a child I was a supporter of Inter Milan. That team had fabled players, like Sandro Mazzola. One day, after I turned fourteen, I realized that I did not believe in either God or Inter. I left both the church and football and I never went back."

* * *

My own foray into big-time soccer journalism almost ended before it had begun. Shortly after my arrival in Chicago, where the opening match between Germany and Bolivia was to take place, I received a fax from Tina Brown. She was on the QE2

162

5

Wilson, Jonathan
NEW YORKER MAGAZINE

WorldCupUSA94™

FIFA

ME³

4357

headed for England, but she wasn't writing to describe her hours on the shuffleboard court. It had come to her attention that both *The New Republic* and *The Atlantic* had already run long pieces on the World Cup without a ball having been kicked. The danger was that *The New Yorker* was about to look belated—especially as I had signed on to write one of those elegant after-the-event summaries that now belong in the Jurassic age. The message was cease and desist. I decided, for the moment at least, to ignore the fax. I had press passes already in hand to games all over the country. The coming month held the potential to be one of the highlights of my life. Tina was on a BOAT. What, really, was she going to do?

On the steaming hot afternoon that the games got underway, I was at Soldier Field with Tina's fax folded up in my back pocket, waiting for Oprah to get things started. Oprah drew our attention to Diana Ross, who was about to take a penalty kick— a version, designed for locals, of throwing out the first pitch. After Diana missed her shot (wide left), Oprah introduced President Bill Clinton, who declared the games officially open. Bill was roundly booed by what I supposed was a largely Republican crowd. There didn't seem to be another explanation; Monica Lewinsky hadn't even been hired yet. The booing of politicians of both stripes was constant during World Cup USA. At the four opening ceremonies I attended—in Chicago, New York/New Jersey, Washington, D.C., and Boston (each venue had its own show)—all local and national politicians, with the exception of Bill Weld, the Republican governor of Massachusetts, were booed simply, it seemed, for being politicians.

Germany beat Bolivia 1–0 in a not too exciting game. The cops were all geared up for hooliganism, but the crowd might as well have been watching lawn bowls: it was as tame as could be. Most Americans, it should be noted, had no idea what was going on in Chicago that afternoon, as ESPN, prime carrier of World Cup 1994, had decided to pass up the opening game in favor of the U.S. Open golf tournament.

Later that night, I was slumped in my seat at the gate at O'Hare waiting for a plane to take me to New York for match day two when I noticed that everyone around me was glued to the TV. It was O.J. He was driving down the highway in L.A., and a fleet of cops was in pursuit. They were going very slowly, as in a parade. Like everyone else at O'Hare, I was engrossed, and then, after about half an hour, it came to me: O.J. was totally fucked, and so was I. There was no way this news wasn't going to get through to even the meanest mariner on the QE2, let alone the Queen of Buzz. Tina might turn the entire next four issues of *The New Yorker* over to O.J.: Jeffrey Toobin was already sharpening his pencils. Even ESPN had cut away from the NBA finals for the chase. The World Cup? Forget it. On the other hand, maybe O.J. was a blessing in disguise: I could fly under the radar, no more faxes. In fact, at this point, I was probably off the radar altogether.

At the Ireland–Italy game at Giants Stadium the next day, a huge crowd of Ireland supporters sang and chanted their way joyously toward the four o'clock kickoff until they were interrupted by the arrival in the center circle of Liza Minnelli. Liza performed a less than compelling number that dampened but could not quite destroy the wonderful atmosphere that had been building. While the music drove to its charmless climax, Liza's lyrics scrolled up a huge video screen: "The candles in our hand … the war we've fought to win," something or other that "brings us pain." Later I learned that the words belonged to "The Day After That" from the musical *Kiss of the Spider Woman*, and had been adopted in 1993 by the American Foundation for AIDS Research as its official anthem. Liza had sung it, quite appropriately, on World AIDS Day, December 1, but it was unclear why she reprised the number for the World Cup. The Irish crowd, briefly baffled, recouped and began to chant, softly at first but then with a force rising to match that generated by Liza's amplifiers, "You'll never beat the Irish!"

Soccer fans love to entertain themselves; this is something my fellow Americans just can't seem to get. Much has been written about the techno-blasts at basketball games and the digital exhortations to NOISE that fake up an atmosphere at most of our major sporting events. What it bespeaks is an anxiety about the ability of sports to entertain in and of itself, and of crowds in particular to generate the kind of excitement necessary to stimulate a recumbent TV audience and stop it from switching to *Dancing with the Stars*. During World Cup 1994, this nascent anxiety was evident in the extravagant pregame shows at the first-round matches. It was clear that the electronic media had forgotten that people in large sports crowds are quite capable of amusing and diverting themselves without plunging into boredom or anarchy.

Wherever I went, fans' efforts to enjoy themselves were further impeded by the constant surveillance of the police and the World Cup's "purple beret" private security force. Soccer's dark reputation as a catalyst to mayhem had preceded its arrival in the U.S., and despite the absence of England's team, and hence its fans, the security apparatus was set up to handle megahooliganism in this peaceable republic where the average person owns between three and nine guns (there are different ways of figuring it out). Outside the stadiums, overzealous guards stripped fans not only of smoke bombs and flares but also of anything that could conceivably be transformed into a weapon—or, as the security people liked to say, "a projectile." Umbrellas and flagpoles were confiscated, along with several objects that it was hard to imagine functioning as anything but themselves: water-bottle caps, apples, bags of pretzels. The *Los Angeles Times* quoted Dianna Valdez, a security guard, judiciously explaining, "You can throw a pretzel and you can hurt someone." I must admit I missed the smoke bombs. A blue-and-orange haze used to be de rigueur at big European games, where it drifted lightly and harmlessly between crowd and pitch. On June 24, I rode on a Brazilian supporters' bus from downtown San Francisco to the Brazil–Cameroon game, at Stanford. The fans were a quiet bunch—families, mainly, the parents conservatively dressed, the kids all sporting Brazilian soccer shirts with the name and number of their favorite player stamped on the back. The only visible gesture in the direction of carnival was a long, glittering gold wig worn by the bus's oldest occupant, a man in his sixties with dark, leathery skin. Staring at the happy Brazilians, I realized that for days I had felt something was missing, and now I knew what it was: fear and violence. If you grow up attending soccer games in England, you are so used to spine-chilling episodes that the adrenaline flow they bring becomes an essential part of your chemical makeup. If I didn't have to cross the road five times to avoid bands of skinhead thugs, or listen in terror as twenty thousand fans chanted "Kill the Yids" or "You're gonna get your fucking heads kicked in," I didn't know I was at a game. Once I realized that my entire soccer consciousness was perverted and that I could get by without terror in the stands, the games in World Cup USA took on an air of sublimity. The English *weren't coming*: it was heaven.

No smoke, no fire. On June 26, after twenty-four games in ten days featuring some of the best international soccer to be seen in a long while, Alan I. Rothenberg, the chairman of World Cup USA '94 (a man who never quite managed to sound as though anything other than the bottom line was on his mind), came on TV at halftime during the United States–Romania game to apply a little spin to his own fears. He reassured viewers that although "everyone was worrying about hooliganism," the World Cup was in fact "a Mardi Gras." When the Mexicans and the Irish had celebrated two days previously, Rothenberg declared, "even the police had joined in." Americans were to put aside their ugly fantasies (engendered, undoubtedly, by what they knew of European soccer) of pitch-invading, referee-chasing, crowd-crushing psychopaths, and join the merry throng of party-animal foreigners dancing in the streets as if every day was Fat Tuesday.

* * *

Despite the lack of crowd ferocity the World Cup had its own scandals brewing. Nothing to rock the earth off its axis like O.J., but enough to complement and buoy the tournament along with the unlikely triumphs of Team USA who, against all odds, kept winning. Enter Diego Maradona, Argentina's legendary midfielder.

Maradona, who grew up in a shantytown on the outskirts of Buenos Aires, is still considered by many to be the greatest to ever play the game, superior to both Pelé and Lionel Messi. But his reputation is not pure gold. In the quarterfinals of the 1986 Mexico World Cup, playing against England, with the echoes of the 1982 Falklands War still reverberating between the two countries, Maradona infamously punched the ball into the net to score Argentina's first goal. It was a handball seen by just about everyone in the world except the referee and his two linesmen. Afterwards, Maradona described his effort as "A little bit of the head of Maradona and a little bit of the hand of God." The entirely dubious "Hand of God" goal was followed in the second half by one of the most extraordinary moments in the history of soccer. Maradona went on a sixty-six-yard run and dribbled around six England defenders before slotting the ball into the net. FIFA later voted this virtuoso one-man display "The Goal of the Century." Argentina went on to win the Cup, beating West Germany in the final. After magnificence, a fall: in 1991, while playing for Napoli in Italy, Maradona was suspended for fifteen months after testing positive for cocaine. Now he was back for one last potentially glorious go-round with Argentina's national team.

In his first appearance of the tournament on June 21, at Foxboro, Massachusetts, Diego swaggered through Argentina's game against Greece, dishing out perfectly weighted passes to his forwards and laying the ball off with deft flicks before capping his performance by sending a hard, swerving left-foot shot past an immobilized Greek goalkeeper and into the top left-hand corner of the net. Eight minutes before the end of a 4–0 rout, Maradona's coach, Coco Basile, pulled him so that—as Basile later explained—the star could receive the ovation he deserved. Before leaving the field, Maradona approached the referee and gracefully extended his hand. The ambush was so effective that the ref clasped and shook before realizing how easily he had been seduced. The huge, Greek-dominated crowd at Foxboro, which had chanted "Maradona prima donna!" throughout the first half and booed the Argentinian every time he was tripped by a defender and awarded a free kick, now offered a smattering of respectful applause. He was Lazarus returned from the grave, nasty coke habit behind him, the pellet gun with which he had spattered some Argentine reporters earlier in the summer tucked safely in a drawer, the hand of God held lawfully by his side.

In his next game, against Nigeria, Maradona turned up the heat, and, in retrospect, he did seem rather sprightly out there, especially for a guy who three weeks earlier had departed some of Argentina's warm-up games shapeless and out of breath.

Sharp back heels, close control, even the occasional longer run that gave you a quick flash of the old, truly sensational Maradona—he put on a show that was histrionic, melodramatic, and compelling. At the end of the game, while the adoring Argentine fans rained down confetti and sang their melodic chant of "*Vamos, Vamos Argentina*," Maradona put his arm around the girl who had come to escort him to the drug test. He smiled, waved, blew kisses to the crowd, and the girl, somewhat bashfully, smiled, too. Four days later (O.J. was in the L.A. County lockup at this point), it was revealed that Maradona had been playing under the influence of an ephedrine cocktail consisting of nasal spray, weight reduction pills, and other esoteric discomfort mollifiers. His enterprise was Faustian—to lose twenty-six pounds in three months, get his legs going, and rewire his soccer synapses. He very nearly succeeded. You had to give it to the guy: it's hard to wave farewell to your own genius. Look at Muhammad Ali.

*   *   *

On July 2, my job was officially saved, this time by absolute tragedy: Andrés Escobar, the Colombian left back, was murdered in a Bogota bar after he had scored an own goal, inadvertently directing the ball into his own net and thereby contributing to his country's elimination from the games by the upstart United States two weeks earlier. It was truly nasty, a calculated killing spawned by the singular concatenation of violence, drugs, gangsterism, and gambling in the infamous Colombian city of Medellín. Escobar's confessed murderer, Humberto Muñoz, was the driver for a wealthy cattle rancher, Santiago Gallón Henao, who, rumor had it, had bet heavily on the Columbian team. Suddenly America's attention, somewhat lackluster to this point, was

170

drawn to the games. Word quickly came from on high to keep going. Of course I had never stopped.

There was a lot to talk about during the 1994 World Cup. The question was, with whom could one talk about it in soccer-hating America? While the stadiums and their immediate environs were authentic centers of soccer life, as soon as you were back downtown—whether in New York, Boston, San Francisco, or Los Angeles—the sense of a knowledgeable, soccer-enthused populace all but vanished. In every other country on the globe during a World Cup, you could talk soccer in any café or bar well into the night and the following morning; in America you had to search out an ethnic enclave—and one that spoke your language.

I found my soccer talk on buses and trains and in taxicabs to and from airports. I spoke to Ghanaians, Ethiopians, Nigerians, Iranians, Mexicans, Russians—a broad spectrum of immigrants, plus numerous representatives of the Latino population. Our conversations, I felt, had an air of secrecy about them, as if we were talking behind America's back. We usually started with the game of the day but were soon, like any baseball fanatic, reaching back far into the past, invoking legendary moments of games seen or only heard about. We "foreigners" were like children trying to capture the interest of distracted, absorbed parents. If Americans couldn't see how much soccer mattered, what hope was there for their broader understanding?

But, of course, they *couldn't* see. For a team sport to mean anything, you have to grow up with it and become attached, stupidly and blindly, to the fortunes of your team, like the spectators at the Argentina–Greece game holding an enormous banner that read MAD AND ETERNALLY FAITHFUL OLYMPIAKOS. You also need a history and context for soccer discussion. As with baseball, you need to know what happened thirty years ago in order for what happens today to have significance. Moreover, it's hard to develop a passion for the game if you never played it as a child. In the decades to come when the kids now playing (all sixteen to eighteen million of them) have become soccer-knowledgeable parents and grandparents, Americans will undoubtedly have the ingredients necessary to cook up a superb soccer culture.

In 1994 my soccer conversations with "foreigners" continued in stark contrast to those I had with "real" Americans. As far as I could tell, among "real" Americans, African-Americans were the group most profoundly alienated from the World Cup. While other groups got behind "their" team—whether Italy, Ireland, Greece, Sweden, or Mexico—African-Americans showed no great interest in supporting Cameroon or Nigeria. Spike Lee did throw a fund-raising dinner for the Cameroon team, but there were no street celebrations in black neighborhoods. The reasons for African-American indifference were not hard to understand. First, Africa is a large continent, and about forty African countries did not make it to the 1994 finals. Second, African-Americans are very American in their taste in sports. I won't forget the look of relief that crossed the face of the cabbie driving me into Chicago when, after we had struggled through a couple of awkward exchanges about soccer (the city had issued a World Cup guidebook to everyone likely to come in contact with tourists and my driver held a copy on his lap), I asked him what he thought of Scottie Pippen's refusal to get off the bench during game three of the Bulls–Knicks playoff series. He shook his head as if shaking out the soccer. We passed a huge mural of Michael Jordan, followed a few blocks later by a poster of His Airness spinning a soccer ball (Michael's image, in those days, was to Chicago what

Lenin's had been to Leningrad before the end of the Soviet Union). "That coach," he replied conspiratorially. "That coach must have said something disrespectful to Scottie."

* * *

I ran into Anna DiLellio on July 5th at the Italy v. Nigeria game at Foxboro. I was sitting a few rows behind George Bush Senior and the Houston Rockets star Nigerian center Hakeem Olaju-won when I saw Anna taking her seat a few rows behind two lines of blue-blazered, blue-shirted officials from the Italian Soccer Federation. As a matter of principle, it seemed, no matter how hot it got at games (and, midsummer in America, it got very hot), neither the Italian administrators nor the male Italian journalists would ever remove their jackets. I thought this was a simple matter of suffering for style, but at halftime Anna explained to me that the men were afraid of drafts. They were worried, she said, about the dangers of shuffling between the air-conditioned hospitality tents and media centers and the humid, sultry stadiums and mixed zones. Italy almost lost to Nigeria that day, but when Roberto Baggio saved them with a last-minute goal and transformed himself from a "wet rabbit" (Gianni Agnelli, his club chairman and the owner of both Juventus and Fiat, had called Baggio a *coniglio bagnato*) into a hero, there was much hugging among the administrators and kissing of bald spots, but still no *deshabillage*.

The previous day, on July 4, the United States had been eliminated from the World Cup by Brazil, and after that, it seemed, America packed it in with soccer until the final, when national interest briefly rekindled. If Tina had told me to drop the assignment on July 5, I might have done so.

On July 10, at Giants Stadium for Germany v. Bulgaria, I met Matthew Yeomans (a Brit) and his American friend Tom, both of whom were covering the games for the *Village Voice*. They were inventive reporters and had already produced a parody in the *Voice* of the hyperbolic Italian newspaper *La Gazzetta dello Sport*. Their soccer page showed a picture of the Azzurri under the banner headline WE WHO ARE ABOUT TO DEFEAT YOU, SALUTE YOU! We had come out of the press tent sugared up on Snickers and Coke, courtesy of two of the Cup's corporate sponsors, and were occupying our spots high up in the press box when a group of German fans on the other side of the pitch unfurled a huge banner that read "IT'S NOT A TRICK, IT'S GERMANY." For some reason this struck us as extraordinarily funny. In fact, on account of it, we were in hysterics for most of the game, as if we were completely stoned, but I don't think we were. After the match was over—underdogs Bulgaria won 2–1— we all rushed over to the mixed zone where interviews were to be conducted, but the *Village Voice* press credentials weren't doing it for the gatekeepers. "It's not a trick," Yeomans said, "it's Germany," and we started laughing all over again.

My sense of the tournament's attenuation in American life depressed me, and on the media bus back from the Meadowlands into Manhattan after the quarterfinal on July 13 between Italy and Bulgaria (which Italy won), all my apprehensions were confirmed in the worst way. I was eager to return to the city in order to watch the Brazil–Sweden game on TV. We had left with plenty of time to spare, but the bus got stuck in traffic about a half mile from the Lincoln Tunnel. On a whim our driver left the main road and got into an even worse jam. When the bus hadn't moved at all for half an hour, he suggested that we dismount and try to take a ferry. The journalists straggled down to the ticket office on the dock, dragging cameras and cases, but, we were snottily informed, there were only four spaces available on the last midtown ferry, and those had been reserved for clients of Paine Webber. There was another ferry point a mile away—if we wanted to try that. We broke ranks and began to resemble characters in one of those European movies from the sixties in which a group of people wander around in some no-man's-land for hours exploring a shared existential crisis. This, I thought bitterly, is what happens when you hold the World Cup in a place where not enough people really give a shit. I stared across the river and felt the rage build. Americans (and suddenly I was not one) had been interested not in soccer but only in their excruciating knee-jerk patriotism (USA! USA!)—that, and boasting about what a good show they'd put on, and how great the U.S. was at organizing big events, and the merchandising. My list of gripes was suddenly endless, and all because I couldn't get to the other side of the river (there didn't seem to be a bar close at hand on the Jersey side, and where was Bruce when you needed him?) to watch my fiftieth soccer match in twenty-seven days.

Eventually, I found a cab to take me through the tunnel, and I arrived at my destination—the Forty-Sixth Street Brazilian street party—with about twenty minutes to go in the Brazil–Sweden semifinal. The police had cordoned off about five hundred prospective revelers inside blue "Do Not Cross" barriers. Little Brazilian and American flags were strung across the street from above the small parade of Brazilian stores: Rosetta Lighting and Electrical Supplies, the Ipanema Restaurant, and, the main focus of our attention, the Emporium Brasil café, where two televisions—one large, one small—had been set up high in the storefront window. When the Brazilian striker Romário scored, the street (or our little fenced-off part of it) erupted into an extended and

175

joyful samba. I inclined to the dance but couldn't help thinking about the scene as it would look from space—much of the world dancing to soccer but on the sleeping continent of North America, only two tiny animated dots, one out in California, and one, cordoned off like a dangerous infection, between Fifth and Sixth Avenues in New York.

*   *   *

Brazil went on to win the final, beating Italy on penalties after extra time. The Rose Bowl was steaming hot, but the game less so. Brazil deserved their victory but sadly it rested on an awful moment for Roberto Baggio, who missed a vital penalty during the shoot out: exhausted, he ballooned the ball over the crossbar, a shot that encapsulated both Italy's frustration and its ultimate futility. Afterwards I saw Anna DiLellio for a moment, her journalistic objectivity temporarily suspended; she was almost in tears.

I went back to my hotel and sat by the pool. Earlier in the day, I had called my old friend Billy Grossman in England just to say "Hey, I'm poolside at the Beverly Hills Hilton. I'm going to be in the press box for the final." He said, "Fuck you," then continued, "Are you coming to the reunion?" "What reunion?" "The Club, you idiot. North West: the thirtieth anniversary reunion game. Hampstead Heath Extension." He gave me the date, then added, "Be there."

I was exhausted. For a month, I had been running on Snickers bars and Coke, and by now I could barely distinguish sugar rushes from soccer enthusiasm. I had been home only for certain games played in Foxborough, near Boston, and I was ready for the end. Still, there was one battle left to fight. Early on the day of the final, ABC News released a poll that looked to me like a godsend for soccer's American critics. It claimed that thirty-five percent of Americans found soccer to be "on the dull side" or "a big bore." Thirty-five percent found it "interesting," but only twenty-two percent said it was "exciting." Yet even a small bore, like the final, had held the power to engage, if not enthrall, almost two billion people outside America. I began to make excuses in my head for the depressing inactivity of the final, but then I realized that the best response to snide sports commentators and gloating soccer haters is to explain, perhaps, but never apologize.

Instant Replay:
The Past as Present

Chapter 16

My mother sits across from me in Bloom's kosher restaurant on Golders Green High Street. This is our second visit in the space of a week to her favorite location for dining out, but she doesn't remember the first one. She always orders the same dish—salt beef and chips—then complains that the portions are too big. Nonetheless, like many people who have experienced deprivations at some point in their lives, which for my mother would include wartime rationing, she clears everything on her plate.

I am in London for two reasons: to research an article I'm writing for *The New Yorker* about British novelists and the eruption in their midst of a controversy surrounding Martin Amis, and to play in the North West London U14 Jewish Boys Club thirtieth reunion game. I have traveled farther than anyone else to participate in the match, and the others involved think I am nuts. My years of exile have turned me into a dangerous deviant: when I suggested via e-mail that we might all chip in some money and deliver the funds to a charity of our choice, I was severely reprimanded, accused of being "American" (which I am), and reminded that we were indeed all "chipping in," but the money was going toward a post-game pub crawl.

My mother wants to know if my sons, who are now twelve and eight, are all right, if they're "tall." Height has always been important to her where men are concerned, a measure of health and success. She's only five-foot-three (minus a couple of inches), and my father was five-foot-six. She chews rather noisily and gets a dab of mustard on her cardigan. I wipe it off with my napkin, which she calls a "serviette." She asks me for maybe the fourth or fifth time in the last ten minutes what I am doing in London. Each time I reply, "I'm here to interview some English writers," and she responds, "Who's paying?" This time, however, she adds that whatever talent I have as a writer I must get from her. At Sigden Road school in Dalston between 1919 and 1924, she tells me, she repeatedly won the poetry award for recitation. One winning poem began "Ye who have loved …" but she can't remember any more. In her last year at school, they gave her the novel *Tommy Treginis* as a prize. "I can't find it anywhere," she says. I first heard of my mother's skills as a poetaster more than thirty years ago, shortly before, anxious about the way my accent was developing, she shipped me off for elocution lessons with a demure lady called Miss Rose.

Doris is in a good mood, perky, cheerful, only vestigially provocative (for her). This has been her characteristic state since her memory loss began in earnest about two years ago. There is a possibility that she is in the early stages of Alzheimer's; her mother and both her sisters died after long bouts with the disease. But my mother is eighty-five, and dementia associated with old age is a more likely explanation for her condition. Her good mood—a function of the disinhibition often associated with senile dementia—is, after a lifetime of sulks and tantrums, a blessing to all. My brother Stephen says, "If someone is cheerful in our family, then you know they must be sick."

We get onto the subject of the car, which I have been designated to bring up by my siblings. I try to explain why it's dangerous for her to continue to drive. She retorts that I'm being ridiculous, she makes one three-mile journey a week, to visit her best friend Hetty Feldman in Cricklewood, and the rest are quick shopping expeditions. She stabs a couple of chips.

"My eyes are perfect," she says.

"But what if you break down?"

"I'm not going to."

"I don't want you standing about in the rain."

Tears start to come into her eyes but she fights them back.

"Look, Mom, eventually you're going to drive up to Temple Fortune"—her neighborhood shopping area—"then forget where you parked."

"Why should I do that?"

"Your memory isn't what it was. You're eighty-five."

"What do you mean? Give me an example."

"Well, if I phone you and then I call you again two days later, you don't remember that I called you the first time."

"When have *you* ever phoned me two days after you phoned me the first time? You phone once, then I don't hear from you for two weeks."

Truth defeats logic. I'm amused to note that her particular mix of wit and discontent is still functioning at a high level. But it's late-in-the-day amusement, only possible because time and distance have let other hurts heal.

Because she continues to be stubborn about the car, I change the subject back to poetry. "What about Yiddish poets?" I ask. "Did you learn any of their work?" In the old days a question like this would have enraged my mother. ("Yiddish? I don't know

Yiddish!") Now, however, with the far past her happiest playground, and her old hard-line attitudes loosening, Yiddish is making a comeback.

"Do you want to hear a Yiddish song?" she asks, and without waiting for a reply, breaks into a few lines of which I can only understand the word *berogus*, which means, approximately, "grudge."

"Why are you *berogus*?"

She translates: "'You're walking around all day with your nose in the ground'—that means 'disgruntled.'"

It is a good song for my mother because she herself has been a great grudge holder, not speaking to siblings and in-laws for years at a time, for so long, in fact, that she would sometimes forget the cause of her initial resentment. But it's not the appropriate lyrics of the song that strike me, rather the refinement and accuracy of that "disgruntled." My mother does a crossword every morning in the *Daily Mail*, still honing her talent for synonyms (she has never been able to answer cryptic clues). Her large vocabulary remains dauntingly intact. Unlike myself and most of my middle-aged friends, who have what my brother Geoffrey refers to as "Junior Alzheimer's," she doesn't appear to stumble or flounder in the language. The events of the recent past slip her grasp but not the words to describe them, perhaps because those words came in at an earlier stage that is still retrievable, or are held in a different memory box, a part of the brain unaffected by her dementia.

She touches her hair in the coy, girlish manner she has always affected. She believes that she was and is beautiful. It is an enviable confidence. "I'm still 'ere," she says, taking a comb from her bag to tug through her thin gray hair. "Still 'ere" has become her mantra. She says it in a mock Cockney tone, the register that she

184

and her friends and neighbors must have used in the 1930s to poke gentle fun at the less educated classes. I can date the play-accent with precision because she is quoting Mr. Oberman, who in the last month of her first pregnancy in February 1934 always, so she liked to repeat, greeted her on the street with a cheerful "Still 'ere, Mrs. Wilson?" In terrifying symmetry the words have returned to mark the passage of her old age.

She is still here, although "here" is a twilight world, a largely substance-less present without continuity. She can no longer read a novel, which used to be one of her favorite pastimes, because the plot is lost to her as soon as she puts down the book. Plot and narrative are increasingly absent from her post-1960 life too, the story of how she got from A to B or what her motives were for doing what she did. Fortunately, she cannot remember that she forgets.

*   *   *

When the waiter takes away her plate she rests her elbows in the vacated space on the table. Her skin hangs loose on what were once sturdy plump arms. Forty years ago she stood in our small kitchen running wet clothes through the wringer and turning the handle with impressive power. This memory was first triggered by an illustration that I came across some years ago while read-ing the popular children's book *Peek-a-Boo* to my youngest son: a woman at the washing machine in her crowded kitchen circa 1945 was my madeleine. Each time I turned to the page I was rushed back to the images, sounds, and smells of North West London in the early 1950s. Now, I cannot let it go.

Memory, as Proust for one made abundantly clear, is fre-quently dependent upon the associations sparked by chance

185

experiences. But for my mother, in her current state, experience itself is too fleeting to act as a catalyst. It takes all her energy simply to jot down the reminders necessary to get her through each day without falling into terminal bafflement and confusion. On her small bedside table next to the phone I found a mountain of notes to herself, including, most recently, a two-week-old stark message concerning her younger sister. "Lena is dead," it says in thick-penciled capitals. Lena is dead, Rene is dead, Leslie is dead, and Harold is dead. "I'm the last," my mother says, a woman of enormous will. You wouldn't have guessed otherwise, even though she is the middle sibling.

I doubt my mother has ever done anything she hasn't wanted to, beyond, that is, the considerable and onerous domestic chores, cooking, cleaning, nursing, duties prescribed by wife- and mother-hood which she viewed, uncritically, as part of her contract with life. Once her husband died and her sons were grown, she turned her intense concentration on what had always been one of her favorite activities: stubbornly refusing to compromise with other people. As befits a member of the Sinatra generation, she has done it her way, which is why she has been so terribly lonely in the three decades since my father died. "I have led a blameless life," she often remarks. She's intelligent enough to indicate through her tone of voice that such an assertion can only be presented ironically, but she means it. How can you be "blamed" when you are always in the right? Unlike my father, who was always asking pardon, usually for things he hadn't done or over which he had no control, my mother has never apologized to anyone for as long as I have known her. This is one reason why her personality remains so oddly unattenuated; concessions sap the will's strength. The old stable ego that D. H. Lawrence says disappeared after WWI remains anachronistically intact in Doris Wilson.

"Why are you here?" she says. This time I alter my response. "To play football."

"Football! That's you. It's all you care about."

"Yes, there's a North West reunion. Thirty years. We're playing at Hampstead Heath extension on Sunday morning."

I tell her who will be there, but my mother remembers the friends of my adolescence in only the vaguest way. She confuses Billy with Mick, Lawrence with Brian. Occasionally she remembers but chooses not to. Whenever I mention my close friend David Friedentag, who died of pancreatic cancer five years ago, she clams up. It's not that she is upset, but rather that she tends to regard other people's suffering (including their deaths) as staking a claim upon sympathy that might otherwise go to her. "Why is the rabbi talking so much about Bertie?" she famously asked at the funeral of her best friend's husband. "He's dead." In the old days when the tragic past of the Holocaust survivors who lived on our street was invoked, my mother would inevitably bring up the day the roof was blown off our house by a German rocket.

She doesn't want coffee or dessert; she has always regarded it an indulgence to order something that could as easily be made in the home. During our conversations I generally try to keep us in the past—she is best in the first half of the twentieth century—though occasionally I can't help but convey a piece of current information too hot to keep in check. So I tell her that Adam is a terrific goalkeeper, that Gabe is a star forward on his soccer team, and then, stupidly, I mention something about my brother-in-law, Jonathan Katz, who is in the entertainment business. Until a few months ago my mother was perfectly aware of all these people, but now she struggles to identify Gabe by name, and Jonathan Katz's familial role needs careful explanation.

"Jonathan Katz is signing a deal," I say, "with Steven Spielberg!"

"Steven Spielberg? Does he still live down Park Avenue North?"

I know instantly whom my mother has confused with the director.

"That was Steven Schomberg."

"With the zipper factory?"

"That's right. It was his father's business."

Later that day, although I feel guilty doing so, I call my brother-in-law in Boston and recount the conversation. An hour after I have spoken to him, Jonathan calls me back.

"I have bad news about the deal," he says, "it *is* with Schomberg."

* * *

When did my animus against my mother collect with as much force as my love for her? The moment that persistently presents itself occurred in the Bournemouth Odeon cinema during a summer vacation in 1960. I, the baby of the family, the only son young enough to hang out with his parents, accompanied them to an evening showing of *South Pacific*. For the first half hour or so, my father was fine; then he began a sporadic, irrepressible cough. Members of the audience began to *tst* and sigh. My mother loudly whispered "Lew" in admonishment. Eventually, before she had had a chance to hear her favorite song, "Younger than spring-time," we left. Outside, I held my father's arm while my mother walked in a white fury beside us. "I'm sorry, Doris," my father repeated. She didn't respond. My father continued to cough up the only tune he knew; there was blood on his handkerchief.

The waiter brings us the bill before I have finished my decaf. They like to hurry you along, and my mother approves because a certain rudeness and haste connote for her a comfortable Jewish ambience.

"Have you got money?"

I put cash on the saucer.

"You all right for money?"

I always answer "fine" to this question, even when I am deeply in debt. My mother is not a stingy person; she is conservative in her spending, but not stingy. When I was growing up I remained blissfully unaware of the financial struggles that were taking place. Later, my brothers enlightened me.

"Don't worry about money. I've got plenty of money. I've saved all my life. Don't worry. You'll get it when I die. I'm splitting it evenly among the three of you."

"Why would you do that?"

She laughs. She likes this kind of slightly mean joke. My eldest brother Geoffrey is a wealthy man. He bought my mother her new house and in an unobtrusive, generous way provides for all her needs.

"You're like King Lear," I add.

"Goneril and Regan."

"That's right."

For a moment I see how the arc of my mother's life has carried her from Dalston as Verona, with young suitors knocking on the door of Shrier's bakery in Shacklewell Lane, to Lear's blasted heath presently substituting for Hampstead's in the foreground of her consciousness.

I drive her home to the small two-bedroom house that she has lived in alone for the past twenty years. It is clear that she can't cope by herself anymore, but she refuses to move into any kind of home, and she makes life an utter misery for those who are employed to help her (punches have been thrown). Sooner or later, no matter how experienced and tolerant, the helpers all leave. Why doesn't she live with one of her sons? It is what she wants. Her best friend is regally ensconced in her eldest daughter's spacious house, but her best friend has a sweet and accommodating personality, and my mother is not only difficult but an active troublemaker, especially between husbands and wives.

"How old am I?" she asks.

"Eighty-five."

"That's what Geoffrey says too," she responds, with a sense of wonder rather than bitterness.

"That's because it's what you are. We're not trying to trick you."

"I'd rather be eighty-four. That's what I tell people."

"Tell them anything you want."

We go in and sit opposite one another in her lounge. A wave of boredom and irritation washes over me, a response to being alone in a room with my mother that is unaltered since adolescence. She adopts her characteristic prim pose: knees squeezed together, back upright, pocketbook held in her lap. I sift through the magazines and papers neatly piled on the sofa. They cover a number of years and are all articles or reviews by or about my brothers and myself.

"How does it feel to have two sons retired?" I ask. Geoffrey, recuperating from a bypass, has decided to put his real estate business aside and take things easy for a while. Stephen, at fifty-one, has taken early retirement from the National Health Service.

"You never started," she says. "You never worked. You're not working now, are you? You made your mind up what you were going to do—not work—then you did it."

When I was younger, I often went to other friends' houses to play after school, but the visits were rarely reciprocated. As opposed to one's own, the parents of friends are notoriously attractive and amenable, but even my *friends* agreed that my mother was impossible. Like the city of Boston, she was fond of banning. In the summer of 1967 alone, she banned from our house Michael Sheldon, whose parents were both Holocaust survivors, because he wore an ankle-length leather coat that she called a "Gestapo outfit" and had the temerity to argue politics with my Uncle Harold; and, after Stephen had married "out of the faith," all gentile females. Prior to my brother's marriage, non-Jewish girls (we never said *shikses*, it was considered vulgar) were permitted to cross the threshold, but, unbeknownst to them, they enjoyed a different meal plan from their Semitic sisters, one that was soup-free and limited to egg on toast.

I wander into the hallway, where the mantel over the central heating radiator displays two small wooden Viking figures that Geoffrey brought back from a trip to Scandinavia decades ago. Their axes and helmets are detachable playthings, but my mother doesn't like them to be touched and warns her youngest grand-children off as she once took them out of my hands. She holds a steady attitude toward most of her possessions: when things are altered, chaos is come. She doesn't want me to adjust the volume on the TV, or change the video in the VCR—since Geoffrey bought her the equipment, it has hosted only "The Three Tenors" (once), and for a brief period five years ago a few loops of my video of her eightieth birthday party at Stephen's home in Oxford. Next to the Vikings—one fat, one thin, a Nordic Sancho Panza and Don Quixote—is a framed photograph of an English folly, Stow Castle, with its façade of sixty-foot high battlements concealing a roof that slopes down to an English country cottage. Geoffrey purchased this landmark English home as a weekend retreat, then sold it after a few years of ownership, but for my mother it remains a symbol of the palatial heights scaled by our family. Behind the picture of the castle is a photo tree on which are hung four snapshots of the beloved men in her life: her three sons and her younger brother Harold. We are all uniformed, two by school and two by the army. She has chosen to exhibit only the cleanest of clean-cut moments. My father's image is nowhere to be seen on the ground floor of the house.

I enter the kitchen. Attached to the wall to the left of the fridge there is a narrow lined notepad that my mother has transformed into the most primitive of calendars. In the middle of the page she has written 1994; curled back on the spiral are the preceding four years, each with a line drawn through them. The kitchen as her own private prison: it's a prop to make Samuel Beckett proud.

"What are you doing in here? You want tea? I can still make tea, you know. I haven't lost my marbles—not yet. What do you want? Biscuits? Or something else? A little sandwich?"

*　*　*

Instead of driving back to my hotel, I am drawn to my old neighborhood. I want to see the house where I grew up and maybe take a walk in Gladstone Park. I stop my car opposite 8 Helena Road. The semi-detached home is, of course, even smaller than I remember and, disturbingly, it is in a state of disrepair. The stones of the crazy-paving front path that my father laid with his own hands are cracked and broken, the front hedges are overgrown, the windows in the garage doors are smashed, and the house hasn't been painted in years.

Next door on one side were Stanley and Lily Fisher, who were English-born Jews like us, and next to them the Gilchrists, who were Lily's parents. Then the Walshes, who were not Jewish and who would not return a soccer or tennis ball if you were unlucky enough to land one in their garden. Then the Belindas, who in 1960 moved from one side of the street to the other after they had a third child and needed more space; they had begun life in England as refugees from Hitler's Europe, like the Bernards farther up on our side and the Preiss family on the other side. There were the Baums, and the Posners, whose son was very fat, and then, on the corner, the Solomons. On the other side of the street were the Roses and the Kutners, whose son Douglas hanged himself in his bedroom after terrible battles with teenage depression, and next to them the Feldmans, whose eldest daughter Doreen later became a baroness, and then the Citrons, who called the police during the only party I ever threw, which took place while my mother was in South Africa in 1969, and next to them some people who owned an Austin A40, and then the Lloyds, who moved to Hampstead after Prime Minister Harold Wilson made Dennis Lloyd a Law Lord, and of whom my father would proudly say "He has two degrees—Oxford and Cambridge," which we would find snobby and worth a laugh. The Lloyds sold their house to the Beckers, whose eldest daughter died of leukemia when she was fifteen; three houses down from them were the Balls, whose daughter Jackie had the same birthday as me, then the Obermans, who used to come and see me in my baby carriage because Mr. Oberman "liked to hear that little boy talk," and the Leafs, whose son Michael once bit into an apple in synagogue when the shofar was blown to signal the end of Yom Kippur, and whom my mother called "Schnippy Leaf" until he married the Preiss girl from six doors down and was restored to his proper name. Then the Morrises, the Sheldons, and one or two more families whose names I can't remember, and finally, back on our side of the street, the family to whom our semidetached was attached, the Heritages, who besides the Walshes were the only gentiles on the street. Mrs. Heritage had multiple sclerosis and was in a wheelchair; Mr. Heritage was a stern disciplinarian of his two daughters, Joanie and Sheila. At night you could hear him shouting at them through the dividing walls in a voice that carried over the shouting in our own house. All these people lived in small, well-preserved homes surrounded by carefully tended gardens on Helena Road, and they are all gone from it now.

In February 1961, on my eleventh birthday, my mother took me to see a rerun of *The Ten Commandments* at the Plaza in Piccadilly Circus. She wore the squirrel coat whose copious sleeves I loved to sniff and bury my face in, although my pleasure was tempered by the knowledge that as fur coats go it was a failure, not mink, and therefore, to my mother, an unenviable sign of the limitations of my father's income. I must have been dressed exactly as she wished, my belted mackintosh over the maroon sweater she knitted herself and covering the coarse worsted shorts that I hated even though she had sown silk strips on the inside at the hemline so that I would not get a rash. My hair must have been combed and parted at the side. For what else can explain the fact that we left the house without either a row or her sitting on the stairs, face in hands, screaming that she will not move until I comply with her sartorial and tonsorial demands. No, everything must have been perfect because I cannot remember any tension on the tube ride, which means that I didn't inadvertently say "bloody" or mention my friendship with someone she didn't like. And I was still four months away from disappointing her by failing to gain admission to one of the direct-grant public schools that held the names of the great medieval guilds: Haberdashers' or Merchant Taylors.' So on this winter journey, for all these reasons, and because of the heavy scented security of that fur coat, I was able to enjoy the smoky allotments by the railway lines, the blue flashes from the rails, the way light snow melted on the train windows and formed streaming deltas there. I loved the plunge into darkness at Finchley Road, the bulb-lit carriages smelling of stale Woodbines, the texture of the bulbous handles on flexible grips when we stood for the last moments of the journey as the tube rounded a curve and jolted into the station. When we finally made it to the Plaza, my mother shook the snow off her hat (I liked the sparkling hat almost as much as the coat) and we went in to the darkness together for what may have been the last time without an element of rancor or bitterness pervading our relationship.

I walk down the street, perhaps trying to get away from these memories, but I only find more. I turn onto Park Avenue North and there is the house that once belonged to the Kelmans, a large, extremely orthodox although not ultra-orthodox, Jewish family. To the astonishment of the entire neighborhood, the eldest son married a Christian girl. His parents covered the mirrors in their house, sat *shiva*, and performed all the appropriate rituals for mourning the Jewish dead. As far as I know, they never saw their son again. In our house the Kelman family's behavior was considered to be extreme, but not incomprehensibly so. I don't know how many dead Jews were walking around London when I was growing up. Sometimes you bumped into one of them at the grocer's or the fishmonger's. They were fewer and fewer as the years went by.

I turn and walk fifty yards to the park. There everything is as it was: the vista, the green, the path to the library, and the two great oaks that formed the first and best goal I ever knew. I traverse the railway bridge and begin to climb to the top of the hill, where I expect to find the cafeteria that once sold lollipops, sweets, and drinks. The building had begun its life as Dollis Hill House, a small, gracious, aristocratic home. Lord Aberdeen, an early owner of the property, entertained Prime Minister Gladstone there, and in the summer of 1900 Mark Twain visited its latest owner, his friend the newspaper proprietor Hugh Gilzean-Reid. Twain wrote that he had "never seen any place that was so satisfactorily situated, with its noble trees and stretch of country, and everything that went to make life delightful, and all within a biscuit's throw of the metropolis of the world." He added, "There is no suggestion of the city here; it is country pure and simple, and as still and reposeful as the bottom of the sea ... Dollis Hill comes nearer to being a paradise than any other home I ever occupied." During WWI the house was used as a hospital, and in WWII Churchill's cabinet met there on occasion. When I arrive at the top I see that all that remains of the cafeteria I knew is a burned-out shell—the result, I later learn, of two fires in the space of three years, probably set by arsonists. I can see all the way down to the synagogue, but that too has lost its former glory. The place is shuttered and fenced; perhaps it will live again as a mosque.

The only Jewish world that ever interested my mother is what my friend the late novelist Alan Isler used to refer to as "the Great North West," that slice of London pie bordered on one side by the stations of the old Bakerloo line between St. John's Wood and Stanmore, and on the other by the stretch of Northern Line that runs from Belsize Park to High Barnet. "I see," the

196

novelist Clive Sinclair wrote to me after a meeting with our mutual acquaintance Will Self, "that we are all smartass Jewboys from North West London." I thought of Nick Carraway finally figuring out what it was that linked the apparently disparate sensibilities of himself, Daisy, Tom, and Gatsby: "[We] were all Westerners, and perhaps we possessed some deficiency in common which made us subtly unadaptable to Eastern life." I had thought myself thoroughly alienated from the England of my childhood, and imagined that I had left for America because a Jew can never *really* be English. It was as simple as that. But this trip was making me realize that deep down I was a North Westerner, a member of that group of people at home in Gladstone Park or on Hampstead Heath, but uncomfortable—"subtly unadaptable"—in Kew Gardens or Richmond Park.

I turn up on Hampstead Heath extension the following morning to play soccer. I am wearing a blue and white Argentina shirt, the closest I can find to the old North West strip. I am crossing the field when I see a small group of men standing under a grove of plane trees, all smoking cigarettes in preparation for their exertions. A couple of them, Laurence Milton and Brian Solomons, look up and spot me. We haven't seen each other for thirty years. "Wilson!" one of them says, "you *fat* fuck." I feel completely at home.

Extra Time

Chapter 17

I did not read Nick Hornby's seminal soccer memoir, *Fever Pitch*, for a long time. Many friends urged it on me, but because it was about Arsenal, I chose to ignore the book. Yet I was drawn to it. In bookstores, I would pick up a copy and flick through; every sentence I read captivated me but my resistance was strong. Eventually I capitulated. *Fever Pitch* is a brilliant piece of writing, and a lot of it is about the pleasures of disappointment with a team, and the pains of disappointment inside a family.

I happened to have an acquaintance, the novelist Roddy Doyle (a Chelsea supporter), who was a friend of the author. I also happened to own half a dozen Arsenal soccer cards circa 1968, the year that Hornby fell in love with his onerously successful team and became a Gooner. ("Gooner" is widely used by Arsenal friends and foes alike to describe a fan of the team, and is derivative of "Gunner"—Arsenal's official nickname is "The Gunners," and their emblem a piece of field artillery.) I had found the cards in a set of 100 in a baseball memorabilia store near my home in Newton, Mass. Allison, the shopkeeper, couldn't remember how she had come across them, and they held no interest for her. She sold me the box for twenty bucks.

After I finished *Fever Pitch*, I sent the Arsenal cards to Nick Hornby. He wrote me the sweetest card, gracious and grateful. Receiving the cards of some of his favorite players from childhood, he said, was one of the best things that had come out of writing his memoir. I was touched, but the imp of soccer rivalry was in me, so instead of letting the exchange drop, I wrote back to let Nick know that really *he* had done *me* a favor. The Arsenal cards, I explained, had been poisoning my collection.

I know it's utterly infantile, but I wasn't joking. I really didn't want the cards. They were terrible karma. When I was in Vegas I had sympathized with punters who stayed away from the Luxor; superstition is endemic in sports as in gambling, and I myself was certainly not immune. I had, over the years, tried to will victories for Tottenham by shaving/not shaving on match days, wearing/not wearing the replica shirt of the Spurs team that won the F.A. Cup and League Double in 1960–61, and so on. It was almost impossible to tell what worked and what didn't, as so many variant factors came into play, but I'm more or less convinced that I was personally responsible for getting Spurs into the UEFA Champions League for the 2010–2011 season by hitting the perfect combination of attire, facial hair, and Hopi rituals the day of Tottenham's vital victory over Manchester City in the penultimate game of the 2009–2010 season.

Not long after dispensing with the Arsenal cards, I saw Nick Hornby give a reading from his novel *About a Boy* in a bookstore in Brookline, Mass. During the Q and A, a provocateur in the crowd asked him how he viewed Arsenal's relationship with Tottenham Hotspur. "Well," Mr. Hornby responded, "they *used* to be our rivals." It was painful, but at the time, it was true. Arsenal had done nothing but great things for decades while Tottenham, after glorious triumphs in the 1960s, had more or less been frozen in an aspic of mediocrity ever since. I felt this barb as a personal assault. If I had been as gracious as Hornby over the matter of the cards, he would surely have replied more generously. But what am I saying? Of course he wouldn't have. He's a Gooner!

Chapter 18

I was standing on the right wing, which is where I always stood, not in politics—in that regard I am more or less a central defender with aspirations to play inside left—but in soccer. The wing is where people in their forties who were once blessed with speed play even when they no longer are. I was once blessed with speed.

It was a bright fall day. I had been advancing and retreating up and down the right wing for about an hour, and the ball had come my way, what, once, no, twice. The first time it was directed by our midfield dynamo, Jacques Paoli, who would die of cancer within two years of making the long, accurate, curling pass that landed at my feet as if directed by a GPS, which hadn't yet been invented at the time we were playing this game, and the second time the ball ricocheted off the fat Peruvian ass of Mario, our diminutive striker. Everyone referred to him as "the Italian," because it was only in his fifth season of playing in our Over 40's league that he got fed up with everyone saying *buon giorno* to him when he turned up at the field and yelled, "I'm not Italian, you fucking morons. I'm from Peru."

On the adjacent field, a game of women's soccer was in

progress. Everyone who was not American-born on our team (including those who had daughters) thought that women's soccer was a huge joke, but the sport particularly seemed to offend Leonid the Russian and Bob (his real name was Ahmed) the Lebanese-Christian, who regarded it as a blight on the face of the earth like Al Qaeda or Rush Limbaugh, although we didn't know about either of them then. We tended not to watch the women's game (which generally started half an hour after ours) because some of them ran faster than we did, and because they all seemed to have their breasts strapped up so tightly in sports bra swaddling cloths that there wasn't any perceptible jiggle at all.

At this point in the game we were down to ten men: Carlo, one of our two center backs, had been sent off for biting the leg of the opposing team's striker, a tall sinewy Swede who had fallen across Carlo's lunging tackle like the swordsman who fell "straight as a pine" in the Japanese forest in Robert Hass's great poem "Heroic Simile."

Our team, Newton United, had reorganized in the wake of Carlo's red card, with Ernie Moniz, our overlapping left back, moving into the central defender, role to which he was quite unsuited, as he was the shortest person available. In his other life, Ernie was the chairman of the physics department at MIT. He had been playing with us for three years before anyone discovered this salient fact, and for all that time his teammates had been yelling things at him like "Hey, Ernie, THINK! Look where you're passing, THINK a little bit!" Then we'd point to our foreheads, indicating where Ernie's brain reactions should take place. Once we discovered he was a theoretical physicist, we stopped yelling "THINK" when he made an errant pass and instead shouted questions at him from across the field like "What happened, Ernie? Did you miscalculate the earth's rotation?"

Ernie was of Portuguese descent, but because of something involving a research lab in somewhere that sounded like "Putt-farken" he had spent a great deal of time in Germany and generally responded to our loopy enquiries by swearing at us in German. According to Ernie we were all "Scheiss." Ernie is presently Secretary of Energy in the Obama administration.

Over on the far side of the field, near a line of forsythia bushes yellow as the shirts of the Brazil national team, our defensive left midfielder, Mike Reznikoff, a crunching tackler and great header of the ball who always wore a swashbuckling, multi-strapped fiberglass contraption to protect his banged-up left knee, was engaged in a tussle over a throw-in with one of the other team's non-English-speaking players. Two years from now, right around the time that Jacques Paoli was diagnosed with cancer, Mike would be killed in a car crash on Route 9, but at this moment what the indifferent universe held in store was not available to us. The forsythia, magnolia, and cherry blossoms had burst and we, despite Carlo's ignominious departure, were winning 1–0.

We were, like Melville's crew of meanest mariners and renegades, aware of ourselves as crewmen while our shore lives remained, for the most part, a mystery. I had no idea what Mike Reznikoff, who had wrested the ball from his boisterous opponent's hands and was launching one of his trademark long throws, did for a living. For the longest time this blissful ignorance went for almost everyone on our team. Aside from Ernie, whose resumé had somehow leaked into the public sphere, everyone's profession remained happily closeted, as if we were indeed the class-free society that America claimed for itself but never realized. In time, information dribbled out during pre-match warm-ups (rub EZ Heat on back of legs) and rainy halftimes: Carlo was a hairdresser in Belmont, Jacques played and taught jazz piano at the Berklee School of Music, Steve Branfman was a potter; but as for the rest of them, Leonid, Hal, Zev and Zevi, Kirk the goalkeeper, who claimed he had once been second choice in the Jamaican national team (everyone in their forties made spurious and dubious claims about their glorious past lives as soccer superstars, but the most far-fetched claims invariably came from Israelis, Jamaicans, Lebanese, and anyone else who hailed from small soccer countries and were thus unlikely to be challenged. I mean, I couldn't exactly declare that I had once played for England without being labeled delusional), the team's off-field lives remained as opaque to me as was my own life to my son's hamster. What we had in common was soccer, and the fact that we were, with two or three native-born exceptions, Americans by green card and late-coming citizenship. This meant that (natives excepted) not one of us had a good word to say about the United States soccer team, with its cozy, irritating name of Team America. We all hated it. We would all have rooted against the U.S. for any "axis of evil" soccer country. Everything else about the place was more or less okay.

Mike Reznikoff's long throw arced down the left sideline, deflected off the knee of one of their defenders, and went skidding along the soft spring April grass for a corner. I stood at the far post waiting for the ball to cross the players in my path and come into the direct line of my forehead, at which point I would, with a deft twist of my head and neck, redirect it into the goal and be showered with gold by my joyful teammates. The fact that I had not scored a goal with my head since 1965 did nothing to dampen the optimism with which I approached the impending corner.

For ten years, I had been playing for Over 40's soccer teams, representing the towns of either Needham or Newton, usually in the second division of the Over-the-Hill Soccer League. Sometimes, one of the teams that I was on got promoted, only to slide down again the following season. Almost all my knowledge of towns within a five- to thirty-mile radius of my own derived from Sunday morning journeys to away games, sometimes even as far as Cape Cod. We played in wind, rain, sun, and shadow against the hidden world of soccer-fanatic immigrants, teams who spoke only Spanish or Portuguese on the field, teams from high-tech exurbs like Sudbury and blue-collar towns like Hudson. Now I was about to graduate to another league, the Over 50's. I didn't have to move on. I could stay in the Over 40's if my legs could handle the pace, which, it has to be admitted, wasn't all that fast. It was the end of the season, and I had to make a decision.

As it happened, the ball sailed several feet over my head like a heavy white bird on its migratory path south. I trotted back to await the goal kick and thought of one of my favorite stories by Chekhov, "About Love," which began: "The next morning there were *pirozkis* for breakfast ..." I loved that this story began in medias res, but so expertly, in that one was magnetically drawn into the story by those three words, "the next morning." It successfully hid a truth about life and time that we humans have tried hard to obliterate with the establishment of artificial divisions like "weeks" in order to give us the illusion that we are the masters of both. In truth, it is an unbearable fact that everything we do takes place in medias res, and that aside from the inescapable brackets with which we begin and end life, there is no start-stop at all.

Hence the distinct appeal of one aspect of a soccer game: its time-freezing illusion of neat containment and finitude signaled by the referee's two long whistles, *there's a freight train comin'*, at the beginning and the end of a game. What is more—and Ernie

Moniz might have had something to say about this, as he had been deeply shocked when I told him, over sliced oranges one halftime, that I had no idea what an electron was—it was my experience (if not my reality) that when I played soccer, time stopped.

*　　*　　*

The fact that it was now raining quite hard made things difficult for Kirk, our Jamaican goalkeeper, for the simple, insane reason that he refused to wear cleats and instead patrolled his goal line in winklepickers, long narrow lace-up leather shoes with a pointed toe. He started slipping and sliding almost as soon as the first drops hit the turf, and then the ball almost went through his legs. He managed to retrieve it, but his ensuing projected punt upfield skidded off the side of his shoe, and in a manner I would have thought physically impossible, actually wound up bouncing behind the goal line for a corner.

There had been some debate on the team about whether or not to buy Kirk a pair of proper soccer boots. I.e., was it possible that Kirk couldn't afford them? I mean, for all we knew, he was homeless, but then again, for all we knew he had just sold his stock in Microsoft and simply preferred to play in regular shoes.

The corner was cleared by a defender's powerful intervention.

I was dallying near our goal (occasionally I went back "to help" at the back in order to show that I wasn't a complete prima donna forward) and for some reason, the ball safely upfield, I decided this was the time to broach the shoes issue. "Hey Kirk," I said, "not so good in the rain, huh," and nodded in the direction of his footwear. Kirk replied, "No man, they're okay." And that was the end of that.

A few minutes later, the ball—that glorious leather orb (synthetic nowadays) so finely celebrated by James Joyce in the early pages of *Portrait of the Artist as a Young Man*: "and after every charge and thud of the footballers the greasy leather orb flew like a heavy bird through the grey light"—which had been bobbing about aimlessly in the middle of the field like a beach ball punched around by a bored baseball crowd, suddenly arrived at my feet with Frisbee-like swerve and speed. I set off down the wing in a dash, or at least it felt like a dash, but apparently did not appear sprint-like to my son Gabriel, who had arrived on the sideline five minutes earlier and was now standing under a purple umbrella with his friend Marisa. When I was brutally upended by their left back (a foul that the referee somehow missed), I heard him say to Marisa, "It's like he's running in slow motion."

Filippo Marinetti's "Futurist Manifesto" of 1909 insisted that it was possible to capture speed in paint: but the distance between theory and practice in both his work and that of his fellow Futurists—Giacomo Balla, Gino Severini, and Umberto Boccioni among them—is hard to miss. I mean, just because you affirm that something is so doesn't mean that it is. In, for example, Boccioni's *States of Mind 1: The Farewells*, an enormous effort has been made by the painter to suggest industrial strength locomotion, but the result is no more or less active than a still life by the seventeenth-century Spanish master Luis Meléndez, whose bread, figs, wine bottle, and oranges don't try to move at all. The Futurists would have been better off plumbing the depths of the spatiotemporal sensations that accompany the aging process. For example, before I was tackled I *felt* like an express train going down the wing, but clearly I *looked* like a stationary heavy goods vehicle.

I got up from the ground. My shirt was now covered in mud, and the proud Alitalia logo that ran across my chest was obscured. We all had blue shirts with the airline's logo and name emblazoned on the front in white. We had received this odd sponsorship because Felice, our sometime striker, was an Alitalia pilot. Work commitments prevented him from showing up to most games, and when he did come he was histrionic and self-parodic, whining and indicating terminal despair with his hands whenever a move broke down. But he had a great head of curly gray Harpo Marx hair and he sometimes scored spectacular goals, and everyone has the right to devolve into their national stereotype from time to time—and he *had* got us the shirts, so who cared if he couldn't stop letting us know that we all disappointed him.

I have suspected for a long time that deep down, Italians hate soccer. They pretend to love it, but actually they hate it. They play not to lose, and their defensive tactics are at once cynical and superb. In 1994 they lost in the World Cup final to Brazil on penalties, which was a relief to everyone except the Italians. Then they got their revenge in 2006 by beating a French team that played lovely soccer and deserved to win, but succumbed to Italian ruthlessness after the great Zinedine Zidane failed to prevent himself from reacting with the famous head-butt to the taunt from defender Marco Materazzi. According to Anna DiLellio, with whom I had remained friends since the World Cup in 1994, Materazzi's provocation was couched precisely as follows: "Your sister is a whore … and everyone in Milan has fucked her."

Now the rain beat down hard and began to soak through my shirt. It had moved from drizzle to torrential in just a few minutes. All the spectators (all five of them, that is, including Gabe and

Marisa) had left the sidelines for the shelter of their cars. Only Carlo's Senegalese girlfriend Jaineba remained. She stood regally under a yellow umbrella. Carlo had disappeared somewhere in a huff following his red card dismissal. I had once said to him, "Why don't you marry her? She comes to every game." And he had replied, "Why don't I marry you? You come to every game."

For a winger, a wet pitch is good—defenders lose their footing, and it is easier to slip by them. I felt I could probably have got past my fullback without recourse to much trickery, but the ball didn't come my way, and probably because of the downpour the referee, a beefy Honduran, blew for halftime at least ten minutes earlier than he should have.

As the rain let up, we stood sodden, drinking from our water bottles and wishing someone had brought orange quarters for us to suck on, the way we did for our children. I was talking to Steve Kadish, who had had a heart attack last season but returned to play. This was a man who had put his life on the line for the team and was thus deserving of enormous respect, although he didn't really get it, probably because Steve was one of the few native-born Americans on the team. He had played in college, for Tufts. He was really good, but nobody wanted to admit this, as to do so would undermine our outlook, ethos, and confidence, all of which were based on the prejudicial notion that no one born in the United States could either understand or play soccer the way it was supposed to be played, i.e., with glasses on, barely running, overweight, oxygen-deprived, and sucking for air, but massively aware of what might be accomplished if only the body would respond a little better to the instructions coming from the mind.

The problem that Kadish's comeback presented for the rest of us was that he had conclusively proved that with the exception of death and paralysis there were really no reasons at all to stop playing soccer.

The women's game was over, the sun made an effort to break through the clouds, and the soft loop of time between halves expired at the referee's whistle. As we were trotting back out, I said to Kadish, "Do you know what an electron is?" And he said, "Yes."

The second half went a lot like the first. Kirk slid around on the wet turf, alarming the defenders lined up in front of him and encouraging our opponents to chance ever more speculative long-range shots; their striker, a ringer for sure, launched shots like missiles. The rest of us walked, intermittently ran, chased, headed, tackled (although in my case not these last two activities, which I tended to avoid), and generally pursued our middle-aged, soccer-playing lives with something very close to genuine enthusiasm. The rain had left the green field sparkling with dewdrops. The game was beginning to wind down; the flock of starlings that circled and swooped above us during the first half departed like a crowd leaving early to beat the traffic, and the sun dipping down through the clouds, impressively Turneresque though it was, appeared to be conveying the message "go home." At this point Mike Reznikoff set off on a dazzling run down the left wing and crossed the ball and I, synapses firing in some last beautiful flare, sprinted thirty yards (okay, twenty) to meet the ball on the volley and crash it into the back of our opponent's net. I raised my arms in triumph. My teammates were too far off to congratulate me. No doubt they would have done so had I made it back to the center circle for the kick-off, but I didn't. When I turned to begin my celebratory run back up the field, my knee popped, quite loudly, and I collapsed in a heap. I wasn't in pain, so two of the other team's defenders simply dragged me to the sideline and dumped me there. The game continued without me. I put ice on my knee and watched as Newton United ran out the dregs of its 2–0 victory. I didn't know it at the time, but my goal was the last I would ever score in competitive or any other kind of soccer.

Because of Kadish and his back-from-the-dead act, leg injuries were entirely discounted as grounds for sympathy. The previous season, someone on a team that only spoke Portuguese had smashed into my shin guard at a point where it met an artery, and my leg had turned black from ankle to knee. I was already on a warning from Sherry, who had told me about a year earlier, "If you get injured again I'm not driving you to the hospital." She had kept her word when I sprained an ankle, and I had driven myself, in great pain, to the ER (it didn't occur to me that I could have taken a cab). She had relented for the blackened leg—after which I had to fly wearing one of those stupid white stockings that look like they belong to Malvolio—but only if I promised I would retire, but of course I hadn't. Now, this popped knee didn't feel so bad (I could walk), but something told me that it was.

A week later Gabe tore his ACL playing in a high school soccer match. We both visited the same orthopedic surgeon, Dr. Tamara Martin, a former boxer and kickboxer. She scheduled Gabe for surgery. Then she turned her attention to me.

"You have a 98% torn ACL."

"Okay, so when's the surgery?"

"There isn't going to be any surgery." Then she said a lot of other things, including "You have cervical stenosis, you shouldn't be out there anyway," that might have sounded persuasive to another forty-nine-year-old who hadn't devoted most of his life to playing and watching soccer.

"Well," I said, "before you decide anything conclusively, I want you to know that the last goal I scored was really spectacular."

"Oh yeah," Dr. Martin replied. "Well, hold on to that memory. You're done."

Chapter 19

In February 2002, I flew back to London to see my mother, whose memory had taken a deeper dip into darkness. I have to admit that I planned my visit to coincide with Tottenham's appearance in the final of one of England's three major domestic soccer competitions, the Worthington (now Carling) Cup. It was the least important of the three competitions—in the years that it was sponsored by the beer company, it had been known as the "Worthnothing Cup"—but I wasn't going to miss it. It had been years since I'd seen Tottenham play.

My nephew James and I had, over a thirty-year period, been intermittently going to games together since he was ten years old, when I brought him to a dour 0–0 draw at Tottenham's home ground, White Hart Lane. Since then, poor guy, he had been hooked. Now he was a season ticket holder, and had procured the tickets for us at the bargain price of $450 each. We were insane. I arrived in London on Friday night; the game was on Saturday. I would have to defer seeing my mother until Sunday.

James and I traveled by train to Cardiff's Millennium Stadium, where major games were staged while Wembley, London's super venue, was under reconstruction. I had not been to a live game in England for several years. The train from London was a "special" exclusively for Spurs fans. The supporters of Blackburn Rovers, Tottenham's opponents that day, would make their way from Lancashire. Even when they are not coming from different directions, opposing groups of supporters are always separated on public transport in order to prevent outbreaks of violence. James, who at the time was the deputy head of production for Channel Four Films, started to make cell phone calls almost as soon as we set off. He was trying to reanimate a deal that was going bad. As the deal in question happened to involve the filming of my first novel *The Hiding Room* from a script by Freddie Raphael, who had written *Eyes Wide Shut*, I had more than a passing interest in his conversations, but I tried to act as if I wasn't listening and couldn't have cared less. The problem was with the attached director, Stephen Daldry, who was blowing hot and cold on the project. Eventually, shortly after I had read on an online rumor mill that Cate Blanchett and John Malkovich were going to star in the movie, Daldry upped the stakes and went off to shoot *The Hours*, starring Nicole Kidman as Virginia Woolf, and everything collapsed. But at this point in time I was still thinking swimming pool/Laurel Canyon.

We got off the train in Cardiff and began the long march to the stadium flanked by cops and separated from Blackburn's supporters. The Spurs fans began a war cry that sounded to me like "YIDS YIDS YIDS." This is because that's what the crowd was chanting. I freaked out. "What's wrong with you?" James said. He looked at me in astonishment. "Didn't you know? We're the Yids!" "How long ...?" I could hardly get the words out. "How long has this been going on?"

The Jewish population of greater London, currently estimated at 283,000, has, since the Second World War, largely been concentrated in North West London, a shift away from both the East End, where the community has its origins, and North London, first stop on the move out of poverty. London's Jewish soccer supporters, while they are divided among a large number of teams with home grounds all over the city, including Chelsea, West Ham, Watford, and Brentford, are traditionally split, in their majority, between Tottenham and their fierce down-the-street rivals, Arsenal. Tottenham's greatest seasons came in the 1960s, although the team generally does well in years ending in the number one (there is a song that marks this unusual accomplishment). Arsenal, although it pains me to say it, have been consistently successful for the last thirty years, not to mention the thirty years before that.

No one has ever taken a body count, but it is my guess that Arsenal has just as many Jewish fans as Tottenham. In the 1960s the Arsenal game-day program took care, come September or October, to wish its Jewish supporters a Happy New Year, and well over the fast. A match scheduled for Yom Kippur was even once postponed out of respect for the team's Jewish adherents. Spurs were never so accommodating. Jewish backing of Arsenal and Tottenham is, of course, only a tiny minority of general English support of the two teams. As with all English clubs, with the exception of Manchester United, which draws a famously fickle international crowd, the teams' fans are primarily from the English gentile and now also Moslem working and middle classes. Nevertheless, sometime around the late 1980s or early 1990s, Tottenham Hotspur became indelibly identified with their Jewish supporters, in a way that I apparently had missed, while Arsenal did not. Perhaps this had something to do with the fact that Tottenham's owner from 1991 to 2001, Alan Sugar, a man who had made his millions from the Amstrad electronics and computer company, was Jewish. But then again, other clubs, including the current incarnations of both Manchester United and Chelsea, have Jewish owners, but they are not called "The Yids." Sugar or no Sugar, rival fans began to heap anti-Semitic abuse upon the Spurs' audience. "Yids" certainly formed part of the vocabulary of insult. In time, the Spurs' fans executed the maneuver favored by many an abused group: they appropriated the insult that had been hurled at them and wore it as a badge of honor.

Nowadays, *everybody*—that is, the team's supporters, its detractors, and neutrals—calls Spurs "The Yids." My brother Geoffrey was once at his gym in London and overheard two Londoners, West Indians both, talking soccer at the next locker. "You watching the game tonight?" one asked. "Course," his friend replied, "I've always been a Yid." On the other hand, the name-calling can easily spiral out of control. At West Ham in East London a few years ago, the crowd began to make gas chamber hissing sounds when the Spurs players ran onto the pitch. The club was warned about its crowd's racist and anti-Semitic behavior by the governing Football Association, but was not fined. This year, they did it again and, to make matters worse, Tottenham fans were badly beaten up in both Lyon and Rome by thugs whose animus appeared to be primarily anti-Semitic rather than soccer related.

In Europe, Spurs are not alone in their Jewish identification. The Amsterdam powerhouse club Ajax is also a "Jewish team." Frequently the object of anti-Semitic abuse, Ajax's own fans chant "Joden! Joden!" Sometimes they go into battle with their rivals under the Star of David. Ajax has hardly any Jewish fans, but prewar the club's ground was, like Tottenham's and Arsenal's, adjacent to a Jewish neighborhood, and hence the affiliation.

In recent years the Football Association, as part of its efforts to stamp out racism in its clubs, have tried to pry the "Yid" label away from Tottenham, and discourage its use not only by the team's aggressive detractors but also by its passionate supporters. It has had almost no success. In the United States when Spurs games are shown on TV, the "Yids" chant, whether by design or accident, comes across as muffled and muted, although certain songs that must be incomprehensible to American listeners do get through. Jermain Defoe, Tottenham's black striker, is always greeted by the home crowd with an affectionate rendition of "Jermain Defoe is a Yiddo." In 2008, a petition circulated designed to press the Oxford English Dictionary into changing its definition of a Yid from the familiar derogatory term for a Jew to "a Tottenham Hotspur football fan."

In Cardiff, all the "Yid" stuff was new to me. To add to my astonishment, as soon as we were safely ensconced at the Tottenham end inside the stadium where seventy-five thousand fans were gathered, a group of Spurs supporters unfurled a huge Israeli flag. "Is this political?" I said to James. "No," he replied, "They couldn't find Israel on the map." Stewards quickly rushed over and removed the offending flag—banners of all kinds were prohibited from the stadium in case they obscured a spectator's view. Tottenham emerged onto the field, at which point the crowd began to beat drums and chant in unison, "Yid Army! Yid Army!" Up the other end of the ground, the fans of the opposing team, Blackburn Rovers, had massed, and they too had something to chant about Yids, but it was not supportive.

The game didn't go well. Tottenham were heavy favorites to win, but they lost 2–1. I had traveled three thousand miles and paid an exorbitant price for a ticket, only to taste the bitterness of defeat.

The next day I went to visit my mother in the nursing home in which she now resided. She had not wanted to leave her own house (who does?), but her situation had become untenable. One day Geoffrey found a young social worker in tears outside my mother's home. When he asked what was the matter, the girl explained that she had tried to convince my mother to wear a safety alert device around her neck, and that my mother had refused. "But Mrs. Wilson, what will happen if you should fall down the stairs?" "Well," said my mother, "I'll die, won't I?" Whenever Geoffrey went to visit my mother in the nursing home and take her out for lunch or tea, she gave him a hard time. Then, one day, he happened to take his car into a car wash while my mother was in the front seat. When they entered the car wash she was yelling at him, and when they came out she was a pussy-cat and couldn't remember why she had been angry. From then on, he only had one immediate destination when she got into his car. He called it "The Brainwash."

"Are you Roger?" my mother asked me. She was sitting in a chair next to her bed, facing her room's picture window, her hair white and thin, her face drawn. I had been turning the pages of an old photograph album. There she was with her sister and family on vacation at Eastbourne, an English seaside resort, shortly before the outbreak of WWII. "No," I said, "I'm Jonathan." Roger, the boy playing in the sand near my mother on the beach at Eastbourne, was my cousin, seventeen years my senior. "Of course you are Jonathan," my mother said, "Do you think I don't know my own son?"

Chapter 20

My mother died in the winter of 2003 at the age of ninety-four, and with her, or so I imagined, went the last residual taboos and restrictions that she had tried to sculpt into my consciousness for half a century. All the wrinkles and creases had been ironed out in more than twenty years of therapy (either a wallet-emptying self-indulgence or a life-saver), and by the age of fifty-three, I was more or less capable of holding a phone conversation while someone else was in the room without too much anxiety that my mother was listening in on the other end. *The Manchurian Candidate*, I always thought, had nothing on my mother, who did not need to plant a miniature electronic device in her sons' brains in order to exert control.

Her memory at ninety-four had been full of holes, like those in her stitches when she stretched out the multicolored scarves that she used to knit. This was the external mother, a tiny, old, old lady with thin gray hair, floating in and out of sleep, all the distant battles, some lost, some won, most ending in a draw, dust and dust, put to rest in a book of ancient history. My internal mother was someone else, robust, still fighting, still saying *No!* in thunder. *That* mother could not be moved a continent away in the manner I had achieved by heading for America when I was twenty-six. I had wanted to say *Yes*, like Molly Bloom at the end of *Ulysses*, yes to experience, yes to border crossing, yes to the forbidden love of gentile girls, yes to the territory beyond the frontier. I thought I had come through.

As it turned out, perhaps it was I who did not know myself, or at least that part of myself still in thrall to the heaviest of all my mother's prohibitions, the one slapped on my father's family: his three sisters, whom she hated, and his distant relatives from Poland, a group so impressively *verboten* that until my mother died I hardly knew—except in the deepest and most unreachable, if ineradicable, parts of my being—that they had actually existed. Only my father's two younger brothers, Simon and Sam, were exempt from Doris's proscription. When I was a child I played with their children, my cousins Connie, who is Simon's youngest daughter, and Ruth, the daughter of Sam. The only child that my father's three sisters produced among them, a boy named Laurence Boxer, was almost entirely unknown to me: the sins of the mothers, which as I understood them included a Polish birth (my father's older sister Fay had arrived in London as a six-month-old babe in arms—"That Pole," my mother called her) as well as envy of my mother's beauty, wit, and charm, were assumed to have filtered down to the innocent son. To play with Lawrence was to risk a series of terrible taints: the stain of old Poland, the stench of poverty, all the tenement miseries of the past.

After she died, my mother's belongings, such as were left to a woman of ninety-four who had spent the last two years of her life in a small room, were divided among Geoffrey, Stephen, and myself. As I do not live in England, only what was easily portable came my way: an art nouveau silver-plate tea set, a small wooden sweet barrel, a 1928–1930 photograph album that had belonged to my father before he met my mother, and, new to me, a cache of letters, two written in German, the rest all sent from my father to my mother in their courting years, 1930–1932.

Sometimes doors open into the family life that you believe you have long ago circumscribed and circumnavigated. So it was when my mother died. For, coincidentally, after I brought these letters and the photo album home with me, a rush of wild information about my family came my way. A few weeks after my mother's funeral, my cousin Connie, who is the director of the Littman Library of Jewish Civilization in Oxford, and who presently, with her husband, the anthropologist Jonathan Webber, lives in Kraków and spends a great deal of time working on issues of Polish–Jewish relations, contacted me with some news that she had dug up about our own Polish relatives and their American descendants. There was, it seems, a second cousin of ours living around the corner from me in Newton, Massachusetts. This cousin, Lisa Samelson-Hattis, was the youngest daughter of my father's first cousin Victor, a person who, until this moment, I had known nothing about.

I called Lisa. She had received an e-mail from Connie and wasn't surprised to hear from me. I drove five minutes to her house. She, her husband Paul, and their two small children had only recently moved to the neighborhood. Their house, a large old colonial on a tree-lined street, was barely furnished; a few toys lay scattered on the wood floor. Lisa was a small woman in her mid-thirties with dark curly hair. I couldn't see any close family resemblance.

We hugged. Lisa made tea. We sat in her dining room and there, on the mantelpiece, my eye caught a photograph of my paternal grandmother, Dora, standing next to a taller bearded man who had his arm around her.

"That's my grandmother," I said, almost as if I were saying, "Are you Roger?"

"Yes," Lisa replied, "with my grandfather. She was his older sister."

"But where was the picture taken?"

"In Poland."

I was baffled. As far as I knew, my grandmother had never left England from the moment of her arrival there as a young married woman in 1905 until her death in 1968. But this was not so. The fact of the photograph and the date scrawled on the back were incontrovertible: she had visited Poland in 1937.

And whom had she visited? The answer came to me twice that month: first, partly, from Lisa, and then, more fully and in another extraordinary coincidence, from my cousin Ruth. Ruth's parents had recently died, and among her father's belongings she discovered a list of names that he had submitted some years earlier to the Holocaust memorial museum, Yad Vashem, in Jerusalem. There were sixty-two names on the list: men, women, children, and babies. There were the names, and next to them the dates of their deaths and the places they had died: Treblinka and Auschwitz. These were my father's and Ruth's father's and Connie's father's close relatives. That's who my grandmother had visited: her eleven brothers and sisters, her numerous nieces and nephews. Not one of our English fathers had ever said a word to us about any of them.

"Your grandmother," Lisa said to me as we sat sipping tea, "lived at 129 Navarino Mansions, Dalston, London, E8. For some reason we all have her address committed to memory."

"But she died before you were born," I said.

"Even so. It was part of Samelson family lore. When my father

224

came out of Auschwitz, this was the address that he wrote to."

Her father was my father's first cousin. *His* parents, my father's uncle and aunt, had died in the camps. There were other survivors, children of my grandmother's siblings, but of Dora's eleven brothers and sisters, unknown to me until this golden afternoon, none survived.

"I know a great deal about you and your brothers," Lisa continued. "I know what you all do for a living. One of your brothers is a psychoanalyst, right? And you all grew up in London. Of course, I didn't know that *you* were in America."

"I'm so sorry," I said, "I don't know anything about you." Later it dawned on me that what I meant was, "I'm so sorry, I don't know anything about me."

What do you do when you are over fifty and history rises up and smacks you in the face? I was a grown-up with grown children of my own. My own present engaged me, but my past, after a long wrestle with the angel, was more or less settled. Grief over my father's early death was in a contained place, while anger with my mother's authoritarian rule had diminished to human comedy. But now I had something new to absorb: my family, which I had believed to be bounded by the cold pebbly shores of the English coastline, had grown exponentially. Or would have done if the majority had not been murdered in Poland. The remnants, as I learned from Lisa, the few who had survived the Holocaust, along with their offspring, were scattered across three continents: in Canada, the United States, Israel, and Belgium.

We sat, my newfound cousin and I, under an antique autumn light filtering through her new home's bay windows. It seemed appropriate for the occasion, as if the maples and oaks of New England had begun their lives as Polish poplars. From a box on the floor, Lisa produced more photographs, and then she began to sketch a family tree.

Behind all she said, behind the dismal family histories with their worn clothes, scuffed shoes, and threadbare lives shunting toward tragedy, I began to detect, no louder than the trees whispering, and sometimes silent as the stars that peppered the sky on my way home, a suggestion of inadequacy or failure on the part of my English family. Nothing was said in anything as sturdy as a word, but rather, in vocal registers and looks that both were and were not concealed. I was familiar with extreme versions of this kind of language (which is known to all) because my mother tended to communicate a minimum of six or seven emotions at a time, almost all of them in contradiction to what she was saying. By the end of my afternoon with Lisa, what should have been a joyous, tender reuniting of lost relatives with a shared wretched past took on the aspect, for me, of something like an indictment. "My family suffered," she seemed to want to tell me, or so I imagined, "and your family did nothing to help."

On my next visit, perhaps in order to make up for something, although I wasn't quite sure there was anything I could have done to change my own part in the past, I brought a small gift for her baby son, Zev, and a soccer ball for her five-year-old, Joey, who Lisa told me had shown an interest in the game.

* * *

In the coming weeks, while all this news of horror and its aftermath was sinking in, my cousin Ruth took a trip to Piotrków Trybunalski, the town in southern Poland which, we now knew, was where our Polish family lived and from where they had been transported to die. From there she mailed me a postcard that read: "Grandma did us a favor getting out. This place is a dump."

226

That was one way to go, I thought, and not necessarily a route to be easily dismissed. William Blake's "Drive your cart and your plough over the bones of the dead" has its merits as a way of living our short lives. Another was to reassess, to look again at the personalities that loomed over one's life, those parents you thought you had down, and see if the picture hadn't been skewed all along. For example, did my father's melancholy, which I had always attributed to the long illness that stemmed from his heart trouble, perhaps have a different or competing source? And there was something else: the letters in German. I needed to get them translated.

My mother, who hated the past and everything old, had her own valedictions forbidding mourning, so much so that, even though she was an observant Jewish woman who ate kosher food and, for most of her life, observed the Sabbath, she would neither light a candle to her husband's memory on the thirty-eight anniversaries of his death that she lived through, nor on the fifty anniversaries of the death of her baby son David, which had surely tortured her throughout her long life. My dead brother whose grave in Willesden cemetery I had never visited. My dead relatives in the camps, who even now, alert to the dangers of unearned piety, I think of as *my father's* relatives and not mine. My mother had one message about the past: do not venture beyond the parameters that I have designated as proper, for there dragons lie, or vulgar Polish Jews, or refugee Jews who do not have English accents, or murdered Jews who will smother us with their suffering, *and what about the roof that was blown off my house in the Blitz? What about us?*

My father too had one message, which was Wittgenstein's as well: "Whereof one cannot speak, thereof one must be silent." One gloomy day in London circa 1959, my father drove me across town to visit an old man in an old people's home. This old man sat in a brown leather armchair and spoke Yiddish. He wore dark trousers, a gray, buttoned cardigan, a white shirt, a silver tie, a light gray jacket, and a yarmulke. He was my grandfather. I sat on his velvet footstool. Perhaps he touched my head. I didn't know his name, and, at the time, nobody seemed to think it important to convey. After about an hour, we left. I had never seen him before and, even though he outlived my father by several years, I never saw him again. *This* absence, it turned out, was simply the tip of the iceberg, or, more accurately, the mouth of the abyss. Suddenly my father's photo album, now singularly in my possession, began for the first time to make sense to me, and so too certain turbulent thoughts, confusions, and memories, some of which had lingered with me throughout my life.

The album innocently documented a walking tour that my father had taken in Bavaria in 1928, as well as a subsequent trip to Belgium. When I was a child, the album was off-limits, though it was not explicitly made so by my parents. I never perused its pages while cuddled up in an armchair with Mum or Dad. I flipped through it alone, without guidance or explication. It contained pictures that ignited my fears of the Holocaust when I was five years old, and it also held the suggestion of a secret: there, in a group shot (undoubtedly taken by my father, although that never occurred to me as a child), were a number of strangers smiling gamely at me from above his neat cursive: "Brussels: When English and Polish cousins meet."

After my father died, my mother hid the album, and I had not seen it again for almost forty years. Now, as a result of the research undertaken by Connie and Ruth, I was able to identify the happy figures who had been my father's relatives.

*   *   *

My father's trip to Bavaria took place over his fortnight's summer vacation in 1928. The first stop on his journey was Nuremberg. *Baedeker's Southern Germany* for that year describes the town thus:

> *Nuremberg, German Nürnberg, a town of 400,000 inhab., lies in a sandy plain, partly clothed with fir trees and intersected by the Pegnitz, which divides the old town into two nearly equal parts, the Lorenz and the Sebald sides, the latter being the older and more interesting. There is no town in Germany so suggestive of an old imperial city as the Altstadt, dominated by the castle, and still enclosed by a wall, towers and a broad dry moat. Nuremberg is also the chief commercial and manufacturing town in S. Germany, machinery, toys, metalware, lead-pencils, gingerbread, and beer being among its chief products.*

My father entered this town of toys, pencils, and gingerbread from the Hauptbahnhof, the main train station, in the dog days of August, en route to acquiring the first of his *Stocknägel*—the little aluminum plaques popular with hikers (they nailed them to their walking sticks) that showed the name and a miniature view of each German town the walker had passed through. His daytime stroll through Nuremberg ended outside the walls of the old fortress. He took a picture there and later, after settling into a small hotel on the Sebald side of the Pegnitz, recorded his first impression of Nuremberg as "a picturesque town resplendent in old world beauty."

It is likely that, at some point during his stay, my father also saw the town's new soccer arena: the Städtisches Stadion, which had just opened that spring. Two years in construction, the

229

stadium was built to be the new home of FC Nuremberg, the local team with a long history of success: between July 1918 and February 1922, it had gone undefeated in 104 matches. The stadium was designed by architect Otto Ernst Schweizer as part of the recently developed sports and leisure park south of the Dutzendteich Lake. The design was awarded a gold medal in Amsterdam (1928's Olympic city) for its exemplary architecture in the Bauhaus style.

The Nuremberg stadium lasted five years as a venue for good soccer—FC Nuremberg won the German Cup there in 1927, in the first match ever broadcast on German radio—before Hitler found a place for it in his plans. From 1933 onwards, it was the preferred marching ground for the Hitler Youth, and it was renamed the Hitler-Jurgund Stadium.

But I will never know for sure if my father saw it in its former glory, as the album makes no mention of it. Among the postcards my father did collect is one of the town's placid river, a few gentle ripples visible on its surface as it meanders between narrow tree-lined banks down to an old stone bridge and tower. It reads, *Nürnberg: Pegnitz einfluss in die Stadt.* Beneath it my father has written: "The Pegnitz—I'm told that in the dim past this river harbored many who had been 'hingerichtet' (executed), but I must confess that by now odors of decomposed bodies have been entirely washed away."

Among the "hingerichtet" were undoubtedly a number of Nuremberg's Jewish citizens. Jews had experienced a rough time of it in Nuremberg more or less from the beginning of their presence there, around the turn of the twelfth century. The commonplace medieval restrictions on Jewish employment and habitation were accompanied by burdensome taxes, protection money, and endless laws enforcing separatist behavior: Jews were not allowed to bathe with Christians or buy eggs or meat before nine a.m., when Christians thronged the market. There was also murder and mayhem, including 698 slain in a single day on August 1, 1298, and 560 who perished at the stake on December 5, 1349. In 1349, a synagogue and the surrounding Jewish houses were razed to make room for a church, the Frauenkirche (sometimes called the Marienkirche). In 1451, a papal decree banned Jews from engaging in commerce, but permitted them to take up certain trades on condition that they wore a yellow ring fastened to their outer garments to alert unsuspecting customers. All this culminated in the Jews' expulsion on Laetere Sunday (the fourth Sunday of Lent) in 1499. Jews did not return to Nuremberg until the beginning of the nineteenth century, when Simon Wolfkehle, a lottery agent, was permitted to take up residence.

By 1928, when Lewis Wilsick arrived, the Jewish population of Nuremberg had reached almost 9,000. However, life for the city's Jews had become increasingly uncomfortable. In 1922 the Nazis began holding their annual rallies in Nuremberg. In 1923, the first issue of *Der Stürmer*, Julius Streicher's notoriously anti-Semitic newspaper, was published there, and would continue to issue weekly vitriol until the end of the war in 1945. There were frequent assaults on Jewish residents, and numerous desecrations of Jewish graves. My father seems to have been oblivious of these events, but he was a young man, and he saw only what he wanted to see: green water meandering through sun-dappled trees.

In fact, my father found a friend in Paul Barth, a local student on his way to a career in the Lutheran priesthood. I imagine the young men found common ground in their mutual immersion in theology, their devotion to music—on the night before my father's return to England, they took in *Otello* at the Nuremberg Opera House—and perhaps their love of the countryside.

Here they were, in Nuremberg, the English Jew and the German Christian. They had met by chance. Sometime during the two weeks of their friendship, Paul brought my father to visit his parents at their home in the suburb of Almoshof. The photograph that marks this occasion shows a couple seated outside at a small, round, wrought-iron table. Herr Barth wears a well-tailored three-piece suit with collar and tie; he is bald and his white moustache and goatee are neatly trimmed. Frau Barth is *zaftig*. In her right hand she clutches either flowers or a handkerchief. At the Barths' feet, on a raised concrete plinth, their German shepherd sits contentedly. Paul's parents seem to aspire to the austere, yet my father's caption suggests an atmosphere more *gemütlich* than uptight: "Paul's parents in the garden of their home ALMOSHOF, NÜRNBERG. 'PHIPPS' the faithful, growing fat from lack of exercise, insisted on being in the picture. SUMMER HOLIDAY—1928."

After my father returned to England, Paul mailed him two photographs taken on his uncle's farm. For a long time I believed that these pictures, which my father placed in the album alongside his own, had been taken by him, and it was only recently that I noticed they're dated almost eighteen months before his arrival in Germany.

The more notable of the two shows a huge sow laid sideways on a long trestle table, trotters tied, teats exposed, dropsical stomach spreading over the edge. Paul and his uncle, both tall and powerful men, stand in work aprons behind the fattened sow. Between them a tiny woman in a white headscarf, possibly Paul's aunt, holds an enamel jug with a broad opening ready to catch the blood. Paul has a knife in his right hand and he grasps it, like a surgeon ready to make an incision, at the sow's neck. A small terrier looks on indifferently. Paul and his uncle smile for the camera from a courtyard strewn with rocks. Behind them stand a rough-and-tumble home, a brick barn, a concrete shed. My father captioned it: "The Slaughter of the Pig—Bavaria 1927. MY FRIEND PAUL ON VACATION AT HIS UNCLE'S FARM—kills his own 'CHOZOR' to make sure it's fresh!" As a child this picture terrified me, for in it the Holocaust was both forecast and recorded.

First the fat dog, now the fat pig. All this happy fattening, this ruddy sausage world, farm and garden in Germany before the war. On the leaf opposite the dog, the domestic scene gives way to the artist Albrecht Dürer's house, now a museum, represented on the postcard that my father glued alone without comment onto a blank page. It wasn't "The Slaughter of the Pig," and it wasn't the unknown cousins, but the house, with its shuttered windows and meanly sloped gables, certainly had its own "Hansel and Gretel" sense of foreboding. I do not know for certain that my father ever entered Dürer's house. But why else would he have purchased a postcard of the exterior and affixed it to a page in his album? For forty years, these images occupied a corner of my mind devoted to all that was ominous and threatening about Germany.

*   *   *

Not long after repossessing the photo album, I had the correspondence between my father and Paul Barth translated by a graduate assistant in the German department at Tufts. All three letters were written in 1948. The first is from a government tracing department in London: Paul Barth had written from Germany, hoping to learn my father's address. The second is a carbon copy of a letter sent by my father to Paul, expressing "joyful surprise" to hear from his old friend after twenty years. What follows is a brief summary of my father's career and family life, and then an extraordinarily understated reference to the war: "Luckily we came through safely but not without strokes of fate." These eleven words camouflage the partial destruction of his house by a German bomb, the loss of his six-month-old son, David, and, of course, the deaths of his sixty-two relatives. My father signs off, "Your still living friend, Lewis."

Paul Barth's response begins with a sigh of relief and a wave of the hand: he is happy to have received my father's letter, and "Your friendly way of writing pleased me too. At times during the past trying years and during the war, I often thought of you and of how you were. I am glad to hear that you survived the war well. It was a bad time." He then gives a long account of his life as an officer in Hitler's Wehrmacht army, fighting first on the Eastern Front, and then, after a short stay in a Kraków hospital for an unidentified ailment (not a wound), in Saxony, where he "fell into American captivity. Already after 14 days I was brought from Pilsen in Czechoslovakia to Nuremberg and was released." The narrative is carefully studded with dates: Paul "became a soldier" in May 1942 and was promoted to lieutenant on "1.1.44." He is careful to say precisely where he was and when he was there. At the end of the war he returns home to find that his car is gone, requisitioned by the German army and never returned to him. This is making life "arduous." He now ministers to two churches and must journey between them on his bicycle. "You see," he neatly summarizes, "that I too experienced a few things." But life goes on: he has thirty-two beehives, he collects stamps.

With its astonishing gaps, alibis, and occasional self-pity, its furtive elision of all that Paul must have seen and heard as an officer on the Eastern Front and during his convalescence in Kraków, this letter is a masterpiece of evasion. Most striking, of course, is the absence of any mention of the fate of the Jews, especially given the fact that he is writing to a Jewish friend. The war has been over for two and a half years; the concentration camps have been emptied of the dead and the barely living. The remnants of European Jewry are spread out in their poverty and misery all over the continent. The Nuremberg trials are still in progress, not too many miles from Pastor Barth's home. But of the Jews, to my father, he has nothing to say.

I sent copies of the letters to Geoffrey, who had turned fourteen in 1948. After he read them, he called me in Boston. To my astonishment he remembered the correspondence. "How did he react to Paul's letter?" I asked. My brother paused for a moment and then said, "Daddy didn't reply."

Chapter 21

In Tadeusz Borowski's autobiographical novel, *This Way for the Gas, Ladies and Gentlemen*, the narrator describes a soccer match at Auschwitz among Polish political prisoners in which he participated as a goalkeeper. At one point, shortly after the arrival of a transport train from Hungary, the ball rolled behind the touchline and Borowski went to retrieve it. What he noted were "splashes of color:" women in summer dresses, men whose white shirts "stood out sharply against the green of the trees." The long procession from the cattle cars stopped and the people in it sat on the grass and WATCHED THE GAME. Borowski took his goal kick. The ball moved from one foot to another and then, as inevitably happens in soccer, it rolled out again behind Borowski's goal and once more he went to retrieve it. "Out of the whole colorful summer procession not one person remained.... Between two throw-ins in a soccer game, right behind my back, three thousand people had been put to death."

Games were played on Sundays at Auschwitz, in all weather, loud and earnest. There was a sizeable group of spectators, hospital orderlies and convalescent patients, and sometimes the crowd swelled hugely for a few minutes when it included the thousands about to be murdered. If you were a political prisoner, you could play; if you were a surviving Jew in the camp, you could not. If you were a Jew you could not have played even if the Nazis had allowed it; either you were on your way to be killed, or you were diseased and starving to death.

I have walked on that field, which was built by the Nazis' slave-labor prisoners, accompanied by a young guide at Auschwitz, the grandson of a former Polish inmate. The goalposts are down, the lines erased: field, ashes. Even at a museum of horror, no one wants to reconstruct a soccer pitch next to a dilapidated gas chamber.

*　*　*

My father's first cousin Regina Samelson was in Ravensbrück and Bergen-Belsen and survived. But it was not until she was in her mid-eighties that, via my cousin Lisa, I became aware of her existence and traveled to Chicago to visit her. I had been told that she was a repository of history, not only her own, of course, but also that of her and my father's Polish family, and she did not disappoint.

Regina was a remnant among the remnant of Holocaust survivors still living in Skokie, a suburb, or "village" as its inhabitants refer to it, outside Chicago. In 1977, American neo-Nazis infamously planned to march there, but were thwarted. The woman who opened the door was tiny, no more than four-foot-ten, smiling broadly and clearly happy to call me "cousin." She spoke with a heavy accent, Polish-Jewish I guess, and quickly sat me down at her dining room table, where she had prepared a light lunch of bagels and lox. We had a lot to say, and after a while I took out a notebook and began to write down the names, dates, and stories she gave me. Regina was an accomplished narrator: she visits classrooms in local public and Hebrew schools to talk about her Holocaust experiences and those of the family members, friends, and neighbors close to her who did not survive. She also owns a rare cache of photographs that she took in the Piotrków ghetto and which, against all odds, was held for her and later returned by a female Nazi guard at the Ravensbrück camp, where she was first taken. Somehow the pictures also survived Bergen-Belsen. One of them, not taken by Regina, shows children in Piotrków "playing" at being members of the Judenrat, wearing the hats of the Jewish ghetto police.

Regina's neat apartment was a few blocks from the showroom/mail order center of Hamakor: The Source for Everything Jewish, and the company catalogue rested on her coffee table. After lunch, while she puttered about in her kitchen making tea, I leafed through its pages, wondering at the extraordinary varieties of Jewish kitsch on offer to the world, including my favorite: a sweatshirt with a faux Latin logo and motto that read "Maven University: Opinion Over Knowledge."

Regina brought tea and a pound cake. She was small but robust in her being, full of wit, will, and strength, and possessed of a lovely wicked laugh undiminished by tragedy and the passing years. As we sat in her front room in Skokie, with the silverplate tea set on the sideboard reflecting the sunset, and the photographs of relatives long dead peering out from their frames as if they might steal one quick look at the life they were missing, I felt like an eager, silent listener in a story by Joseph Conrad. There was always that moment when Marlow began his narrative and the outside world, bustling London on the banks of the Thames, began to recede and dissolve, while in its place came the forest primeval. Regina had been in that forest, and in the camps that were hidden in it.

She was seventeen when the war broke out and living in Lodz, Poland, the textile center of the country. Her father, Shalom, and her older brother, Fischl, were master tailors. After the Germans took Lodz, Shalom and Fischl were put to work making suits for the occupiers. In February 1940, aware that the Jews of Lodz were about to be crowded into a ghetto, the family left by horse and cart to join their relatives in Piotrków, where the first ghetto had been established in 1939—at least they would all be together. They traveled by back-country roads, but at the border between the Reich and Occupied Poland (Lodz had been annexed as part of the Reich), they were stopped by German soldiers; Fischl was beaten up and one of his hands slammed in a door. In Piotrokow, in the horribly crowded ghetto, survival was again made possible through Shalom and Fischl's skills with needle and thread. They made more suits for Nazi bureaucrats and bürgermeisters. Regina was sent to work in a factory that provided wooden furniture with glass tops for the Wehrmacht army. The Samelson family survived a few roundups and transportations from the ghetto, but then a change in command occurred, and officers arrived who were unfamiliar with the special relationship that the tailors had with their German clients. On October 21, 1942, Regina's parents and her brother Fischl were deported to Treblinka. Regina returned home from her factory work that day to find their apartment empty. She remained in the ghetto for two more years, a slave laborer for the Nazis: the Wehrmacht needed furniture. In November 1944, Regina was taken to the Ravensbrück concentration camp, a site of medical experiments and starvation where, on Thursdays and Fridays, there was no food at all. She worked as a slave laborer, picking potatoes and walking a mile or more every day to deliver her load. They slept three to a "bed," constructed of narrow wooden slats. Other inmates wanted to share with her because she was so small. In February 1945, she was transported to Bergen-Belsen. Anne Frank was in the adjacent hut, but she didn't know her. Starving and close to death, Regina was liberated there by the Allied 21st Army Group, a British-Canadian unit, on April 15.

*   *   *

When I left Regina's apartment, I felt a dizzying sensation, the past collapsing in on me, the missing bricks from the house of my father's life. The taxi back into Chicago took me past the newly reconstructed football stadium at Soldier Field, whose redesign had received so much criticism that it had been delisted as a national historic site. It was, of course, where my World Cup adventure had begun in 1994, and perhaps because I was in a doleful mood I began to reflect on the dark side of the sport I loved and the places in which it was played.

The secret history of soccer stadiums is disturbing. Too frequently, they have become dictators' favorite places to imprison, torture, and murder. There was Nuremberg, of course, but also other more recent abhorrent transformations. In Chile, after his military coup in 1973, General Augusto Pinochet used the National Stadium in Santiago as the center of his roundup operations. There he staged the bloody beginnings of a "cleanup" of leftist opponents and supporters of the democratically elected president, Salvador Allende, which would lead to thousands of deaths, among them that of the immensely popular singer Victor Jara, whose guitar-strumming hands were broken before he was machine-gunned down.

In Kinshasa, Zaire, in what is now the Democratic Republic of the Congo, the brutal dictator Mobutu Sésé Seko tortured and imprisoned opponents in concrete detention cells beneath the 20th of May Stadium—a fact conveniently overlooked by Muhammad Ali, George Foreman, Don King, and everyone else involved in their spectacular Rumble in the Jungle fight in 1974. One of the terrible side effects of Ali's remarkable and courageous victory was the champ's apparent endorsement of Mobutu's government: a stamp of approval that in all likelihood allowed the dictator to strengthen control at home and improve his image in the world at large. Though it must be said that Mobutu's anti-communism had always guaranteed staunch U.S. backing, despite the fact that his repressive tactics reportedly frightened even the CIA.

More recently, Saddam Hussein's sadistic son Uday, once the head of Iraq's Olympic Committee, oversaw the torture of Shi'ite soccer players on the Iraq national team who had failed to meet his exacting standards. His hired thugs beat and caned the soles of the soccer players' feet. Uday reportedly kept scorecards with written instructions on how many times each player should be beaten after a poor showing. One Iraqi defector reported that jailed soccer players were forced to kick a concrete ball after failing to reach the 1994 World Cup finals. Another claimed that athletes were dragged through a gravel pit and subsequently immersed in a sewage tank to induce infection in the victims' wounds. After Iraq lost, 4–1, to Japan in the quarter finals of the 2000 AFC Asian Cup in Lebanon, the team's goalkeeper, Imad Hashim Hassan, along with defender Haidar Jabar and forward Qahtan Chatir, was held responsible for the loss, and eventually flogged for three days by members of Uday's "security" force.

The ghosts in these abused stadiums are almost impossible to exorcize. Institutions built for imprisonment, torture, and murder, like Auschwitz or Robben Island in South Africa, where Nelson Mandela was imprisoned, can be torn down or simply left to stand as empty monuments to their victims. But soccer stadiums used only intermittently for horrors are not so easily destroyed or transformed into memorials, for they are also places where high innocent dramas have taken place, and continue to occur.

Galway Kinnell's poem "On the Tennis Court at Night" begins like this:

> *We step out on the green rectangle*
> *in moonlight. The lines glow,*
> *which for many have been the only lines*
> *of justice.*

The same could be said of the curves and straights of any soccer field, which makes the use of their lines as parameters of injustice and cruelty all the more sorrowful.

In a brave and admirable attempt to recognize and also transcend the past, the German Football Federation refurbished the Nuremberg stadium for the 2006 World Cup finals. In 2001, the federation supported an exhibition, "Fascination and Terror," at the nearby Documentation Centre at the Nazi Party Rally Grounds, which addressed "the causes, the context and the consequences" of the Nazi rule of terror.

* * *

I went back twice more to see Regina on that visit. Each time I was rocked anew. I loved the new Chicago, with its shiny silver

Bean, hip restaurants, and Frank Gehry concert pavilion, with its roof like knights' helmets trailing stainless steel ribbons. I loved best the view of the pavilion from the Art Institute's new wing, from which it appeared through a voile curtain, and light trapped and held by the pale glow of day turned it delicate and mysterious. I was heading toward the Chagall *America Windows* when I saw a display of books that happened to feature the small biography of Chagall that I had published the previous year. Under normal circumstances I would have been delighted, but on this particular occasion I had come to the museum to clear my head, which was full of the darkest of Regina's tales. I stared at the books as if I had no relation whatsoever to their author.

Chapter 22

Beginning with the qualifying rounds, I blogged about the 2010 World Cup for the online newspaper *The Faster Times* which, full disclosure, was then edited by my son Adam. I didn't go to South Africa; rather, *The Faster Times* employed me as an armchair correspondent, and when I say "employed," I mean I made $6.47: my cut from advertising revenue accrued via hits on my page. At the time I couldn't figure out Paypal, and donated the money back to my employers.

I watched from my living room on a not particularly big screen with a narrow red, white, and blue England scarf around my neck until it got too hot. I was not at all an objective commentator in the way that journalists are supposed to be. National affiliations are profound in soccer, although they are generally not as deep as allegiances to a local club. For example, if there is an Arsenal player on England's team, I generally hope that things go badly for him, even if it means potential disaster for England. If an England goalkeeper who is also Arsenal's goalkeeper miskicks in some embarrassing fashion and lets in a goal (as, in fact, the Tottenham goalie Paul Robinson did while playing for England against Croatia in 2006), I would be delighted, as the error would provide me with ammunition in arguments with Arsenal fans for approximately the next ten to fifteen years. As it happens, there were no Arsenal players in the 2010 England World Cup squad, so my club-country loyalties were not tested at all.

I am a U.S. citizen and I could, of course, have chosen to support the USA in South Africa, and indeed I might have done so in almost any sport except soccer. I had grown up with England as my team and I couldn't let that go. This was not stubbornness on my part, and in fact it is utterly commonplace for immigrants to the U.S. to stick with their soccer country of origin. This is one reason why the soccer picture in the U.S. is so muddied. Team USA undoubtedly has considerable armchair support, but whoever those supporters are, they generally don't take time off to attend a game if one comes their way.

The United States national team rarely plays a true "home" game—that is, one with all the advantages that accrue from a rabidly partisan crowd cheering you on. This is an acknowledged problem. In Chicago, Polish-Americans cheer for Poland; in Boston and New York, Irish-Americans support Ireland; and all across the country, Central and South American immigrants, both legal and those cruelly uninvited Cinderella illegals, fill stadiums to yell their lungs out passionately and vociferously in opposition to Team USA, the representative of their new and once much-longed-for home—a place, however, where in an orgy of global exceptionalism, most people have baseball diamonds on the soles of their shoes and gridirons in their hearts.

The response of the United States Soccer Federation has been to move vital games to the whitest and least ethnic neighborhood they can find, which frequently turns out to be Colorado. Sometimes, for CONCACAF games against archrival Mexico, the object is to get as far away as possible from Mexico, Mexicans, or

245

anything resembling the Mexican climate. On the surface it seems like a sorry state of affairs not to be supported in your own country. But is it? Perhaps a case can be made for the open society in the U.S. that allows for both local patriotism and sentimental attachment to the old country. Politicians exhibit an acceptable measure of dual allegiance all the time, although they are not, of course, allowed to root against U.S. sports teams. Fascinatingly, the agonies and ecstasies of loyalty and betrayal are only manifest in men's soccer—the U.S. women's team does not have to play its international games in Colorado.

*   *   *

When I wrote about soccer for *The New Yorker* in the last years of magazines available only in print, the sensation was of talking to a half-empty room. A few over-the-top blogs for *The Faster Times*, and I might have been addressing the passionate, engaged throng at a Barcelona–Real Madrid game. The blogosphere, I quickly discovered, is a wild world. I was generally pleased with the responses I received to my early reports—especially one from Spain that simply said "Great piece!" followed by what I assumed was more heaped-on praise, in Spanish. Unfortunately, it turned out that what Antonio from Valencia had actually written was "Great piece! You fucking faggot you know nothing about soccer."

One advantage of covering World Cup 2010 from my armchair, in which, for the most part, I sat solitary and immutable like a Thomas Bernhard character at a party, was that I could do it more or less undisturbed. Once, the Italian writer Carlo Levi called the novelist Giorgio Bassani, author of *The Garden of the Finzi-Continis*, to praise his latest work. To Levi's surprise, Bassani was impatient to end the conversation. Afterwards, Levi realized that he had phoned during the televised broadcast of a game between Real Madrid and Bassani's team, Juventus. Levi wrote, "That so disinterested and abstract a passion as that of viewing a distant match could win out in the heart of a man of letters or a poet, over the love of self and the paternal passion for one's own work, seems almost incredible." In the end he decided that Bassani's behavior was a "rare and exemplary account of how this civilization can offer incredible results of humility and modesty." I doubt that, but to love soccer more than oneself, to wish to watch a vital game rather than hear one's novel praised: I understand Bassani completely. I sat in my armchair and opened my eyes and heart to the screen. I didn't take notes, as I had done during the 1994 games. Instead I adopted more of an analytic position, allowing the games to wash over me while I attended the action with intense scrutiny, although at other times, I have to admit, I was in more of a dream-like state.

I often watched with the volume turned up high in order to create an atmosphere, but during tedious games I turned it down so I didn't have to hear the vuvezelas, the yellow plastic horns which, wildly favored by the home crowds, produced loud monotone notes throughout the World Cup. When blown simultaneously by tens of thousands of spectators, the instruments seemed harbingers of a planet-wide invasion of killer bees.

Another advantage of watching from home was that I was unlikely to get caught up in either pre- or post-match violence, although on one occasion I almost instigated some myself. My down-the-street neighbor Roberto, originally from Rome, had brought his ten-year-old son Alex over to watch one of the games. Alex, naturally supporting Italy, had several unkind things to say about England and, as we were losing at the time to

Germany, I wasn't too pleased. Roberto intervened and told Alex that if he said one more derogatory thing about my team I would probably kill him. Of course I wouldn't have!

Almost as soon as the games began, it became clear to me (and millions of others) that the England team wasn't going anywhere: the players were exhausted by their long domestic season, and seemed completely devoid of class, skill, and imagination. In the quarter final against Germany, the England midfielder Frank Lampard scored a wonderful goal but, even though the entire watching globe and TV's electronic monitoring devices saw that the ball had hit the underside of the crossbar, then traveled three feet over the line before mysteriously bouncing back into play, the referee and his linesmen failed to notice, and the game carried on. The glaring ineptitude of the officials didn't matter much in the end—England would have lost anyway—but this awful moment somehow encapsulated the lethal disappointment that England carried in its DNA.

About the time that England was eliminated and I was in a slough of despond, I grew bored writing about the games and decided to reinhabit the persona of Diego Maradona, who was ineptly functioning at the time as the coach of Argentina. In the run-up to the World Cup, during the qualifying rounds, I had written a few pieces for *The Faster Times* in the guise of Maradona and had a terrific time, for, as he had done throughout his career as a player, he provided wonderful copy. For example, during the qualifying games Maradona shot at a group of journalists outside his home with an air rifle, injuring four. He got into a spat with no less a personage than the President of Brazil over whether or not it was good for players to have sex before games. And he accounted for Argentina's narrow victory over Uruguay by declaring, "The bearded man [God] came to visit the stadium of the river." It was irresistible stuff.

Was God watching? It seems likely, as over the last decades, God appears to have developed a consuming interest in the world of sports. He often helps individuals toward triumphs and rewards. Christians in particular seem to benefit from God's help, as attested to by the rash of pre-match and post-goal celebrations that incorporate making the sign of the cross. Since the lifting of the Iron Curtain, one of whose functions was to keep God out, genuflection has become almost de rigueur among the footballers of Eastern Europe, and this was in evidence in South Africa whenever Slovenia or Slovakia took the field. Protestants in Western Europe, it must be said, don't thank God nearly as much as either Eastern European Christians of various denominations or Catholics worldwide, and this may be why England hasn't won the World Cup since 1966 and, by extension, why the People's Republic of China, despite its massive population, can't seem to put together an eleven that can beat the Faroe Islands. One thing is for sure: God doesn't seem to like losers much, and they never thank him. I have yet to see a goalkeeper cross himself after the ball rolls through his legs.

As Maradona, I wrote a letter to Tiger Woods offering some advice from a man who had been through the wringer once or twice himself; delivered some halftime speeches in Diego's new role as coach; and excoriated my (that is, Diego's) enemies in the press. These pieces attracted a satisfyingly broad international audience, not so much on account of my writing but because Adam wisely partnered them with irresistible images, e.g., a snapshot of an obese Diego in singlet and Bermudas, or a half-naked woman with the Argentine flag painted on her breasts.

Off the web, soccer talk was much better in my neighborhood than it had been at any time prior. All kinds of people, including lots of natural-born Americans, most of whom I ran into at the small supermarket near my house run by a delightful Russian-American couple Yan and Irina, wanted to discuss the games. There is now a generation in the U.S. that has grown up with soccer, if only as a second-tier sport with a third-rate league to represent it. Even local TV registered the shift: the games were thousands of miles away, yet every night local news broadcasts sought out ethnic communities attached to one team or another and showed them partying. The tenor and availability of soccer conversation is vastly superior to what it was when the World Cup was played in the U.S. in 1994. General knowledge of the game is also markedly improved. Yet there remains almost no soccer talk on sports radio and limited coverage in newspapers, although the *New York Times* is improving. In my own local daily, the *Boston Globe*, its chief sports writer and provocateur Dan Shaughnessy continues to vilify and lampoon the game.

And here I have to admit a prejudice of my own: I don't take seriously what people with an American accent (except my sons) say to me about soccer. This is entirely unfair of me, and I want to change, but somehow I can't. The young Nigerian, Umaru, who works at the pharmacy counter at CVS starts to talk to me about soccer and I am all ears. My American neighbor offers what is probably an insightful analytical comment, and I switch off. As it happens, I have occasionally been on the receiving end of an identical accent-to-sports-ratio prejudice. I used to go to a gym where there were always conversations in progress about football, baseball, basketball, and hockey. If someone asked "Hey, d'you see that game last night?" and I responded that I had, and then in my continued response offered enough words for my accent to be identified, a stunned silence would ensue, as if I had just dropped in on a broomstick from Hogwarts. A similar bias is revealed if I should happen to discuss baseball with my students. The fact that I have been going to Red Sox games for more than thirty years—almost twice as long as some of them have been alive—does nothing, from their point of view, either to establish my credibility or reify my authority. And I understand, I really do.

* * *

When Gabe was young, we used to go to Foxboro to watch the New England Revolution play in the Major League Soccer. The stadium, built to accommodate 60,000, barely hosted 15,000 for soccer matches. The majority of the seats were inaccessible, blocked off by long vinyl sashes. The quality of play was adequate, but nothing more. Superannuated players from the European leagues joined hopeful South and North Americans in a kind of cold fusion, something everyone hoped would be a breakthrough in the U.S., but which never really happened. But none of this mattered. We had a great time, bought programs and shirts, ate hot dogs, and so on.

In October 1996, when Gabe was ten, the first MLS Championship Cup final was held at Foxborough. For this occasion the crowd was expected to swell to acceptable proportions, but on the day of the game a downpour of unimaginable and ceaseless ferocity threatened to wash the event away. Yet the game was not called off, and we decided to go anyway. We bought new raingear at MVP Sports, ponchos with hoods, and wore two layers of supposedly water-resistant sweat pants. Even so, we got soaked through to the bone, but we didn't care one bit. D.C. United beat the L.A. Galaxy 3–2 after extra time. We stood in the deluge and exalted.

I thought of that afternoon as I observed the vuvuzela artists in the crowd at Port Elizabeth. It was winter in South Africa and pouring rain, but fans were undeterred. Germany vanquished Uruguay 3–2, securing third place on a ragged field. The next day, Spain deservedly won World Cup 2010, beating a brutal and cynical Dutch team 1–0, just as Paul the Octopus had predicted. I watched from the Bernhard armchair. At some point during the final, I had a revelation: I missed being out on the terraces, a practice I had abandoned since Tottenham's disastrous loss to Blackburn when my mother had been sliding toward the end of memory. What's more, I missed being out on the field. The ambitious schoolboy dreaming of soccer glory still resided somewhere inside me after half a century of soccer immersion. I was envious. I was sixty, my right knee was shot, and I hadn't kicked a ball for eight years, but I wanted to play.

These days, thanks to ESPN and Fox Soccer TV's superb coverage of the English Premier League, I mainly watch soccer alone on Saturday and Sunday mornings, sometimes from an armchair, sometimes perched on an exercise bike. When Tottenham are at home, my nephew James calls me from the stadium at White Hart Lane and holds up his cell phone so I can hear the crowd chants, which are bleeped out for sensitive American ears. I feel a bit like Dennis Hopper in *Hoosiers* when he was in rehab and listening to high school basketball on the radio. But that's okay. "We are Tottenham," the crowd sings, "We are Tottenham, super Tottenham, super Tottenham from the Lane." Goosebumps every time.

Post-Game

The first goal I ever scored that truly elated me was a header in the playground of Gladstone Park Primary School. The cross came in from the right and I rose, instinctively rather than intentionally, to meet the worn tennis ball with my forehead. The ball sped past the outstretched hands of the goalkeeper, between the green netball stand and an invisible post a few feet away, and smacked into the chain link fence that served as a net. I was seven. The fence shimmered in the October sun. A teacher came out and rang a hand-bell; break was over.

The sparkle and glisten of the goal stayed with me for the rest of the day, and clearly it has never entirely left me. Via soccer I know the world differently: people I would never have met, places I would never have gone, conversations that would never have begun, otherwise occluded or lost domains all open for exploration. It is the associative patterns and passions of soccer that hold me the most: ink-blot skies over delirious crowds, quirky moments, drama, beauty, sublime incongruity. I think of the Chinese blogger in Beijing who wrote from a soccer supporters bar, Paddy O'Shea's, on Dongzhimen Outer Street, happily innocent of North London historical memory, "Here we can

sing and cheer like the Yid Army at the Lane." Or, the agile boys
I saw last May playing in a Venice campo near the Rialto using
the thick marble ornamented pillars of a church as goalposts, the
ball slammed up a step, over mosaic paving and into the church's
massive wooden door as if with the profane goal of demanding
entrance.

Deep in my heart, where it all began, are Sabbath Saturdays
in the 1950's and early 1960's, when, towards the end of the
morning service at Dollis Hill synagogue, the congregation
would begin to get impatient if Rabbi Rabinowitz appeared to
dawdle through prayers. The rabbi, aware of the emergent rest-
lessness, sometimes took a moment to scold us. "I know that
some of you have your cars parked nearby," (orthodox congre-
gants all were supposed, like my father, to walk to temple) "I
know you want to be on your way to Arsenal or Tottenham," he

would glare and tug his prayer shawl tighter around him, "But do you have time for the Mourner's Kaddish?" Silence, murmurs, a glint of heavenly approval in the form of sunlight through stained glass. As I left the synagogue I could already hear the feverish cough and spurt of engines turning. Suburban houses in the distance seemed suspended on the horizon like a faraway big city against the smoky background of a red sunset. My father held my hand and we walked down a narrow path bordered by nettles and dock leaves. I turned my head like Lot's wife; there was the convoy of cars, bull-nosed, all moving up the hill toward the great diversion of soccer.

Parts of this memoir first appeared in slightly different form in the following publications: *The New Yorker, The Paris Review Daily, Agni, Maggid, The Jerusalem Review, Who We Are, Promised Lands, The Jewish Quarterly* and *Jbooks*.

Acknowledgments

Thanks to supporters from:

Tottenham: James Wilson, Gabriel Wilson, Adam Wilson, Sharon Kaitz, Michael Stephenson, Lawrence Gerlis, Michael Sheldon.

Other teams: Ben Wilson (Oxford United) William Grossman (West Ham) John Bailey (Sheffield Wednesday) Josip Novakovich, and Nicolás Livon-Navarro (Barcelona) Timon Stähler (Bayern Munich) Clive Sinclair (Luton) Mike Emery (Crystal Palace).

Management: Jennifer Alise Drew, Gail Hochman, Stephanie Duncan, Anne Putnam, Ellen Golding.

Referee: Richard Charkin

A NOTE ON THE AUTHOR

Jonathan Wilson's fiction, essays, and reviews have appeared in *The New Yorker*, *ARTnews*, *Esquire*, *The New York Times Magazine*, *The New York Times Book Review*, *Tablet*, *The Times Literary Supplement*, *Best Short Stories*, *The Best of Best Short Stories*, *The Paris Review Daily*, and *Best American Short Stories*, among other publications. In 1994 he received a John Simon Guggenheim Fellowship. His work has been translated into many languages including Dutch, Hebrew, Italian, Polish, Portuguese, Russian and Chinese.

Wilson is the author of seven previous books: the novels *The Hiding Room (Viking 1994)*, runner up for the JQ Wingate Prize, and *A Palestine Affair (Pantheon 2003)*, a New York Times Notable Book of the Year, Barnes and Noble Discovery finalist and runner up for the 2004 National Jewish Book Award; two collections of short stories, *Schoom (Penguin 1993)* and *An Ambulance is on the Way: Stories of Men in Trouble (Pantheon 2004)*; two critical works on the fiction of Saul Bellow; and a biography, *Marc Chagall (Nextbook/Schocken 2007)*, runner-up for the 2007 National Jewish Book Award. *Kick and Run* is his eighth book and his first work of memoir.

Wilson currently lives in Massachusetts, where he is Fletcher Professor of Rhetoric and Debate, Professor of English and Director of the Center for the Humanities at Tufts University.